Overcoming Perfectionism

The Key To Balanced Recovery

Ann W. Smith

Health Communications, Inc.
Deerfield Beach, Florida

Ann W. Smith
Caron Family Services
Wernersville, Pennsylvania

Library of Congress Cataloging-in-Publication Data

Smith, Ann, W.
    Overcoming perfectionism/by Ann W. Smith
        p.   cm.
    Includes bibliographical references.
    ISBN 1-55874-111-9
    1. Perfectionism (Personality trait) 2. Co-dependence
(Psychology) I. Title.
RC569.5.P45S65   1990   90-4793
616.85'2 — dc20   CIP

Publisher: Health Communication, Inc.
              3201 S.W. 15th Street
              Deerfield Beach, Florida 33442-8190

Cover design by Graphic Expressions

DEDICATION

To my own private cheerleaders, my parents, my sisters and my children, I thank you.

CONTENTS

INTRODUCTION

After conducting months of research on perfectionism, I discovered two new pieces of information. One, I had more than my share of perfectionism. And two, I was probably crazy to write a book only perfectionists would read. Despite a long period of agonizing about doing it *just right,* I found myself relaxing. I am now grateful for the experience and hope to continue to lighten up with myself.

Among my agonizing perfectionistic thoughts is the irrational belief that it is possible to write a perfectly original book with thoughts no one has yet conceived, and also that I must give credit to anyone who has ever influenced my thinking before I can write about it. This thought continues: If I do give credit, what if I forget someone? If you can relate to this thought, then this is the book for you!

I have worked in the addiction and co-dependency field for over 16 years and I have had many wonderful training and treatment experiences. Many professionals doing similar work with co-dependents are developing a body of knowledge regarding co-dependency and all of its ramifications. We are all in this together and have so much yet to learn. If we're honest, we agree that the real source of our knowledge is the sharing of adult children of dysfunctional families.

The information in this book is drawn in large part from my professional work. But my most meaningful source of information was my own personal journey and ongoing recovery. I have certainly learned more by doing, falling down and getting up than I have ever gained from reading or attending workshops. Writing this book was another adventure in that process.

In my present role as Corporate Director of Family Services at Caron Foundation, I am actively involved not only with the treatment process but also in a supervisory capacity. I work with a healthy and challenging staff. I have found that my perfectionism simply does not work around healthy people, which I greatly appreciate. I have another very significant role in my life as parent to two children, ages 7 and 17. My life with these two beautiful people has taught me that being human and imperfect is all they want or need from me.

My inner life has often been less manageable than my outer appearance. I am one of those people who has always been good at faking it, hoping my insides would eventually believe it. My perfectionism was always more in my self-talk than in my actual performance, until recently. My flaws and feelings have gone public. In a way, that was progress. I have become less able to pretend and am more likely to be doing, feeling and thinking, about the same thing.

I have found that the more openly I express those critical voices in my head, the less I have to listen to them. My support system gives me honest, more objective information than that crazy committee in my mind, and I can begin to put some new ideas in there. It is my hope that this book may serve that purpose for you as well. I hope it will allow you to reframe your perfectionism so that you may be able to keep what's useful and replace the rest with something better. Enjoy the process!

1

The Superhuman Syndrome: Compulsion And Co-dependence

Perfectionism is a fairly common phenomenon. It is quite natural for most of us to strive to overcome our human imperfections. Very few people actually enjoy making mistakes or exposing their flaws, nor do they appreciate the value of the learning experience. This tendency is exacerbated by a society, which feeds the belief that we can and should improve on any flaw — whether in our laundry detergent, skin tone, parenting or lovemaking.

We are told by the media, the workplace, school systems and even our families that we must always do our best. Messages such as, "Anything worth doing is worth doing well" have reinforced the notion that if we can't do it extremely well, why bother?

Overall there is nothing terribly wrong with trying to be the best self we can be. Excellence as a *choice* can be very rewarding. This desire to be superhuman only becomes a problem when we begin to believe that perfection is actually possible — and even necessary — for self-esteem, peace of mind and acceptance by others. At that point it has become a compulsion.

Compulsive Behaviors

Every human being with a minimal degree of honesty would probably identify some form of troublesome compulsion in their lives. We are inclined to repeat any behavior that feels good, even if the feeling is only temporary. Some of these compulsive patterns such as eating disorders and chemical dependency, have a physiological component and may be more accurately termed addictions.

Addicts have a physical craving and dependence on the substance as well as a psychological need or compulsion. Addiction is believed to be caused by a combination of genetics, brain chemistry, metabolism and environment. It is potentially fatal and has severe negative consequences. It is necessary for addicts to detoxify before they can begin psychological recovery.

Compulsion, on the other hand, has been defined as "repeated action without choice."* Compulsion may or may not have a physiological component.

When we become uncomfortable, sometimes consciously, sometimes without even realizing it, we turn to familiar behavior

---

In this chapter I make a distinct connection between co-dependency and perfectionism, along with many other compulsive behaviors. I feel it is necessary to clarify further the distinction between this and the psychiatric diagnosis of Obsessive-Compulsive Disorder (OCD).

OCD is a serious, debilitating form of mental illness believed to have a physiological basis. Its victims have what is termed by Judith L. Rapoport, M.D., a "tic of the brain." Among its symptoms are compulsive hand washing, obsessions with numbers or "checking" over and over without cause. Rapoport also calls it the "doubting disease," since no amount of reason or reassurance will put to rest the belief that it is necessary to check the door the gas or the lights one more time.

Obsessive-compulsives aren't particularly perfectionistic in most areas of their lives. Often their illness focuses on a specific behavior, such as how they enter a door or whether or not they are clean. The only way to stop the mental obsession is to perform the act again and again. Those seeking further information about OCD may benefit from reading The Boy Who Couldn't Stop Washing, *by Judith L. Rapoport, M.D.*

patterns to distract us from our discomfort. It is unusual to find an individual who struggles with only one compulsive behavior. We all seem to have our favorites, those on which we most frequently depend, and perhaps a few we reserve for special occasions, such as when we're happy or depressed.

Working, shopping, cleaning, smoking, exercise, sex, relationships, caretaking, religiosity and gambling are only a few of the most common compulsions. Most of these are harmless, and many are enjoyable. The problem comes when we do them because we have no choice.

For example, Joseph was in excellent physical condition due to daily jogging and workouts at the fitness center. Exercise was a very positive factor in his life until it began to replace other things that were once important to him — like family time, his marriage and work advancement — and despite several injuries, he persisted in his training. Eventually Joseph no longer had any choice over his compulsive behavior. What was once a pleasure became a driving need. Joseph was not aware of this decline until his marriage was destroyed.

Joseph, like many people, denied he had a problem. But in fact denial is part of the problem, particularly when our compulsive behavior is rewarded. Joseph was admired by his friends who described him as a healthy, disciplined, attractive man. He was in good health. Only his family was aware of the negative progression of his behavior.

Occasionally, a crisis will cause the addict to stop abruptly and go into a period of psychological withdrawal. During this time he or she may experience sudden rage, depression, sleeplessness or a dramatic change in energy level. The feelings that the addict had been medicating with the compulsion now rise to the surface and seem to have no cause or explanation.

This is what happened to Joseph. At this point he had three choices: resume his exercise, find something else to be compulsive with or feel his discomfort and work through it. Most of us are so unconscious of this cycle that we instinctively find something else to ease the tension instead of exploring the deeper problem. Fortunately Joseph chose to feel. In therapy he was able to work through the source of his compulsion and gradually let it go.

Connection To Co-dependency

The term *co-dependency* has begun to provide an explanation for many issues faced by people who grow up in unhealthy family systems. At the National Forum on co-dependency (held in September 1989 at the First National Conference on Co-dependency in Scottsdale, Arizona) I joined a group of noted experts in the co-dependency field who developed the following definition:

> *Co-dependency is a pattern of painful dependence on compulsive behavior and on approval seeking, in an attempt to gain safety, identity and self-worth. Recovery is possible.*

Co-dependency is an adaptive response to living in a crisis-filled or stressful environment. It can be compared to growing up in a war zone: You learn the survival skills you need but when the war is over, you find it very difficult to function without the stress.

The stress can have a number of sources: chemical dependency (probably the cause of the greatest epidemic of family illness in our society), mental illness, poverty, physical illness, disability and so on. Although the illness of co-dependency was originally identified through contact with children of alcoholics, it has become clear that it is not unique to that group.

My book *Grandchildren of Alcoholics* addresses the multi-generational aspects of co-dependency. When a family has become co-dependent due to an identifiable stress, such as alcoholism, they will unknowingly parent in that adaptive way, providing their children with the skills of a war zone. The children will suffer from co-dependency with or without the identifiable stress. This co-dependent pattern of behavior will continue for generations until it is identified and treated.

Co-dependency does not only present itself in families with severe stress. Many families learn to correct some of their antisocial behavior and conform to certain expected moral and social standards. They may imitate whatever they perceive to be normal from television or the neighbors.

Where one generation may have been physically or even sexually abusive, the next generation may adapt by going to the opposite extreme and looking very functional. This is often called the Looking Good family because of its seeming health, but some very important ingredients of a healthy family are missing. (Chapter 6 gives a complete definition of the healthy family.)

The severity of an individual's co-dependence depends on many variables. Even within the same family, individuals will have varying responses to the stress. Here are some factors to consider:

- The nature and severity of the abuse
- Birth order and circumstances at birth
- Relationship with the abuser
- Outside supports (such as grandparents or friends)
- Gender and what that means to this family
- Size of family — having more children than can be cared for; being an only child
- Environment — poverty; social stigmatization
- Genetics — which parent you resemble: how you respond to pain; whether your defenses are pretty (as in the perfectionist) or ugly (as in the rebel), your innate survival skills

Not all people who grow up in dysfunctional families are equally damaged. In fact some individuals who have been exposed to extreme abuse may actually look better than those who have not. I believe that even though their outward response may be very different, however, internally their feelings and low self-worth are similar. We also cannot assume that the person who looks healthy and has a successful career necessarily feels good about any of it.

Signs Of Co-dependency

Co-dependency has its origin in early family experiences. The pattern can be identified and described in both children and adults who are no longer in the original stress. Signs of co-dependency include having an external focus, repressed feelings, being comfortable with crisis, boundary conflicts, isolation, tendency to physical illness and compulsive behavior.

An External Focus

Co-dependents depend on people and things outside of themselves for internal feelings of self-worth and a sense of identity. At first we believed that co-dependency had something to do with a particular relationship that made you co-dependent on that person but time has shown that individuals who are in emotional pain, feeling abandoned and unloved, will seek comfort in any form, from anyone.

Although it may seem that they prefer to get all their needs met from one person (often a very dysfunctional one at that), co-dependents show similar signs of dependence in all relationships, including work. Because they are used to getting their needs met only occasionally and very inconsistently, they become accustomed to waiting for crumbs to satisfy their emotional needs.

Co-dependents often live as victims of circumstance, waiting for things to change so that they may feel better and get on with life. "Things" may mean "my husband's drinking, my mother's illness, my financial crisis, my son's delinquent behavior, my best friend's emotional crisis, my own depression, my broken furnace, my work pressure" or all of the above. They truly believe that external events are responsible for how they feel.

Since co-dependents do not have a strong sense of self, they seek validation of their existence and worth from outside. This may come from a relationship — "If you love me and never leave me I will be OK"; or from work — "I'll die if I lose my job." Many women develop a strong identity from motherhood and suffer serious consequences when their children begin to pull away. Many very successful people, particularly those in the helping professions, rely on their profession to define who they are.

Robert, for example, had been a successful salesman for many years, despite his alcoholism. He often felt that his addiction to work (although he didn't define it as an addiction) was more of a concern to his family than his drinking. He enjoyed living on the edge, never knowing what his income would be or whether or not he would make it at all. When he was on top, he felt high, motivated to do more. When he didn't make his quota, he was devastated and depressed.

Robert had become dependent on his work for his self-worth, a pattern that continued long into his recovery from his alcoholism. A crisis during one of his down periods almost caused him to relapse. At that point he was ready to face his co-dependency.

Healthy people with good self-worth and identity have a solid foundation from which to operate. They enjoy love and approval and success, but do not crumble without it. Their good feelings come from the inside, not from the external people and things which surround them.

Repressed Feelings

One of the survival skills of dysfunctional family members is to learn to deny their own feelings. When they are in pain (which they are not permitted to acknowledge), several things may occur:

- They may feel the pain, but use masks to cover it. Some use a smile, others use anger or depression. Internally they believe the mask to be safer or more acceptable in this family.
- They may deny the pain, telling themselves it isn't that bad and that the situation doesn't really bother them. The pain is then absorbed physically in their bodies, or they become depressed or behave aggressively, even abusing others.
- They repress the entire experience, eliminating both the memory and the feelings about it, at least for a while. The feelings often will return in the form of

unexplained nigthmares, anxiety or depression, without any of the details.
- They shut down emotionally and don't feel anything. Even the physiological responses, such as flushing of the face and butterflies in the stomach, may disappear.

In a healthy family these tools are rarely necessary. In the dysfunctional, painful family there may have been generations of this type of adapting, thereby providing no model of appropriate expression of feelings.

Nancy's mother was manic-depressive. She suffered from extreme mood swings where she would be charming at one time and violent at another. Nancy was a very bright little girl who would adapt to this emotional chaos by reading her mother's signals and responding accordingly. She believed that anger meant rage, and sadness meant months of depression. She was determined not to lose control as her mother had.

Nancy became very intellectual. She got wonderful grades and functioned exceptionally well until she began dating and attempted to have a relationship. Here Nancy was emotionally illiterate. She did not feel what other people felt and could not be intimate. Nancy did not know that she didn't know, and until a crisis in her adult life lead her to treatment, she was doomed to isolation.

When the potential of abuse or abandonment is ever present, it is wise to hold one's feelings in and — even when they are clearly felt — to not express them. When we use the word dysfunctional in describing a co-dependent, we must be aware that repression is a "functional" survival tool within the stressful family. Only when we attempt to connect outside of this system do we encounter great difficulty and appear "dysfunctional."

Comfort With Crisis

Co-dependents are surrounded with stress and unaware of its impact. There are several reasons for this chaos. One, childhood modeling provides the expectation that life really is crazy and they should not be concerned when things appear out of control to others. They have normalized stress.

Another factor is the need to quiet the pain internally. Chaos provides a convenient distraction when we would prefer not to dwell on the problems in our lives. While we're waiting for people and things to change, we might as well stay busy.

A case in point is a former client Barbara, who was 28 at the time I met her. She was beginning counseling because she felt it would help her co-dependent mother. Her father was an alcoholic, and he and her mother had recently separated. Barbara was her mother's "best friend" and sole emotional support. She took her mother to Al-Anon meetings because she was afraid to drive and listened endlessly to her mother's detailed stories about her alcoholic father.

Barbara claimed to be detached from her mother and had a busy life of her own. She lived in an apartment with a roommate who was physically disabled with Multiple Sclerosis. She had the responsibility of driving her roommate to work, shopping and providing companionship for her. Barbara worked as a caseworker in the county welfare department. She was excellent in her job, showing great compassion and patience with other people's misfortune.

Barbara was not aware of the crisis in her own life because she stayed continually focused on the lives of others. Only in treatment when away from those she cared for, could Barbara get in touch with the rage of her childhood and the grief for the neglect to which she had become so accustomed.

Other typical stresses of co-dependency include:

- Volunteer work, church, self-help groups, hospitals.
- Association with friends and family members where the relationships are problem-centered — "I give and you take."
- Friendships with needy people where the co-dependent feels unable to set limits, believing, "They need me, so I can't say no."
- Primary relationships with co-dependents, people with chemical dependency, compulsive disorders or mental illness.
- Children with emotional or physical problems.

- Enmeshment with family of origin or spouse's family of origin.
- Living with constant interference and meddling.

When confronted with this list in early treatment, the co-dependent is certain that these demands are imposed from outside. They feel they are victimized by the demands of others. In recovery, however, they learn that there is a time to take care of oneself, as well as a time to reach out to others. The key is to balance these times.

Boundary Conflicts

According to Rokelle Lerner, a noted authority on co-dependency, "Boundaries are our sense of ourselves and our perception of how we are different from others physically, intellectually, emotionally and spiritually." An individual with boundary conflicts will alternate between being a pursuer/invader, or an evader of another's boundaries.

In their efforts to get comfort from others, they may smother, take hostages or become very demanding and possessive of those close to them. This is boundary invading. When they feel smothered and fearful of intimacy, they may run away, physically or emotionally, and become unavailable to others. This is boundary evading. Many co-dependents do both.

Lynn was the third child of two adult children of alcoholics (ACoAs). Both parents had been abused in childhood and were determined not to expose their children to the same. Despite their efforts, however, they could not teach her what they didn't know.

As an adult Lynn found herself bouncing from one extreme to the other in relationships. She married two alcoholics. The first was outwardly abusive and demanding, the second was very passive and withdrawn. In the first relationship she found herself distancing for protection. In her second marriage she was the pursuer of a person who would not participate in the relationship.

Lynn had never had the opportunity to develop healthy instincts about when, where and to whom she wanted to get close. Co-dependents allow abusive people in and prevent healthier people, capable of intimacy, from getting too close.

It is not unusual for a co-dependent to have a history of abusive relationships, in some cases even several incidents of sexual abuse. They do not invite it, but they do not see it coming and have no tools with which to prevent it.

Co-dependents also exhibit boundary conflicts by:

- Not choosing the individuals with whom they wish to relate, letting others pick them.
- Doing someone else's job, assuming responsibility that is not theirs.
- Role reversals — becoming friend to their child, mother to a parent, boss when they're not paid to be.
- Overextending — trying to do too much with limited time and energy.
- Being unable to say no, even in sexual relationships.

The ability to establish boundaries, coupled with a strong identity, are necessary ingredients to healthy relationships.

Isolation

By the time they reach adulthood, most co-dependents have determined that the world is not a safe place, that people on the whole cannot be trusted and that it is much wiser to take care of oneself than to be set up for disappointment and hurt.

This belief has been reinforced over and over. Co-dependents also have come to believe that they cannot depend on their own perceptions to be accurate. So, to avoid humiliation, and hurt, they keep things to themselves. It is very possible that an individual may develop excellent social skills and be surrounded by people, but he or she will be isolated internally and truly not known to others. Lynn, for example, had many friends, but in recovery she realized that none of them really knew her.

Their isolation is supported by unconscious feelings of shame and fear of abandonment. Many secrets are kept with the fear that, "If I am found out, I will be abandoned. If you abandon me, since there is no 'I' without you, I will die."

This isolation has been modeled and taught in their families by such rules as, "Don't tell anyone family business," "We can do it alone," "Don't ask for help outside the family." Children of alcoholics often disclose that even though they and their siblings witnessed the same painful incidents in the family, they were not able to share this information with each other, much less with anyone outside of the family. Many report having conversations 20 years later where they ask a sibling, "Did you see that?" regarding an event that happened when they were five.

Suzanne describes herself as a perfectionist and a caretaker in her relationships. She is very good at focusing on the needs of others and always assumes the role of the strong one. Although she has many friends, most of them are very dependent and don't even ask how she is. They assume that she couldn't possibly have any problems since she looks so well put together.

Occasionally Suzanne has a bad day and would like some support. She calls a friend and asks, "How are you?" hoping in vain that during the course of the conversation the friend will notice the depressed tone in her voice. She then goes to work, dressing as nicely as ever, and buries herself in her duties. She actually performs a little better than usual. At lunch her co-worker asks, "Are you OK? You're a little quiet today." Suzanne answers, "Oh, I'm fine, just a little overwhelmed with work." The conversation quickly returns to the needs of her co-worker.

Suzanne has been trying for years to get love and approval from others by being good and taking care of them. She had hoped that they would reciprocate out of gratitude. They believe she is fine because that is how she looks and what she says. Ironically the thing she fears most — abandonment and isolation from others — is exactly what her behavior is bringing about.

Many of the efforts to overcome shame, such as perfectionism and caretaking, create an impression that co-dependents do not need anything. Their "goodness" puts people at a distance, since others feel inadequate in comparison.

Physical Illness

Three main factors contribute to the tendency of the co-dependent to become a victim of stress-related illness: self-neglect, not setting limits and repression of feelings. If we are focused on the needs of others as priority, we often do not take proper care of ourselves. The true victim/martyr actually believes she earns points in heaven for self-sacrifice and at the very least draws a little attention from those who say, "I don't know how you do it!"

Staying in a stressful environment without setting any limits is natural for the co-dependent, but it takes its toll physically. People exposed to stressful conditions over a long period of time eventually will develop physical symptoms such as ulcers and chronic back problems.

The feelings we do not express are absorbed in our bodies. Repressed anger may surface as teeth grinding, overeating or depression. Unexpressed grief may some day become cancer. Some studies indicate that discharge of old emotional pain can actually prevent illness and bring about improvement from existing conditions.

Other examples of stress-related illness include sleep disturbance, eating disorders, gastrointestinal problems, allergy, asthma, headaches, chronic fatigue, chronic pain and lowered immunity.

Compulsive Behavior

I have never met a co-dependent who did not have serious problems with compulsion. It is clearly a tool used to medicate pain, and it works. Perfectionism is one of the compulsive behaviors symptomatic of co-dependency. To overcome perfectionism the co-dependent must thoroughly address his or her co-dependency, while at the same time learning healthier patterns of living.

Overt And Covert Perfectionism

Perfectionism is not as easy to identify as many of the compulsive behaviors mentioned above, since it often expresses itself subtly in all areas of life. It affects not only our behavior but also our beliefs, our attitudes and even our self-talk. It may be very visible or known only to the perfectionist.

The Overt Perfectionist

We all know the person in our lives who is a visible perfectionist. He or she always seems to appear very well put together — self-disciplined, neat, orderly and thorough. Judy, for example, kept everything in her purse anyone might ever need: scissors, Kleenex, comb, a sewing kit, aspirin, nail file, tweezers, band-aids. Her hair was always perfect, as were her children. The spices in her kitchen were alphabetized. She never forgot a birthday, was always on time and had the most organized desk in the real estate office where she worked.

Bill's perfectionism was reflected in his perfectly clean car, washed by hand (didn't want to scratch it) every Saturday. In it he kept a litter bag, maps, travel log and directions to wherever he went, all filed neatly in his glove box. He also kept gasoline mileage and service records. His shirts always faced the same way in his closet; his sock drawer was arranged by color and style.

On the job as a car salesman, Bill was the detail person, the one who thought of everything. He worried about what *might* happen in every situation, offering contingency plans for any eventuality. His work space was extremely organized and he had special pens and markers for certain types of work. He began each day with a list of "What I Will Do Today" — and he attempted to do it all!

Many perfectionists keep their homes in consistent order (the Felix Unger syndrome). No clutter, no waste (many even recycle), a place for everything and everything in its place. Schedules may exist for most daily activities — Monday is shopping, Tuesday is ironing. Even garbage looks good.

Their physical appearance may be meticulous, though a bit fussy, with a great deal of attention to cleanliness, neatness, the right starch in the shirt or a perfectly matching scarf with every outfit.

The overt perfectionist looks totally functional and may even serve as a model whom others emulate. It is not unusual, however, for overt perfectionists to be perfect in one area and chaotic in another. They are attempting the impossible and are bound to break down somewhere in their lives. For example, home may be crazy, while work is flawless.

Overt perfectionists are usually aware and perhaps embarrassed by their compulsion to some degree. They may have a desire to loosen up, but without giving up control. Their issues are very apparent to those around them, who may feel very inadequate in comparison. It is common to find the overt perfectionist surrounded with others who are very spontaneous, with no discipline or order, who provide balance.

The Covert Perfectionist

Covert or "closet" perfectionists are quite difficult to identify. The compulsion to be perfect is more apparent in their thinking than in specific behavior. Although they may focus more on one area than another, the belief that "I *should* be perfect" prevails in most areas.

On the job, covert perfectionists play it safe. Since they believe everything must be just right, they take few risks. When they do try something, they do it so cautiously and thoroughly that it is exhausting, and they vow never to do it again.

Procrastination and indecision also may be problem areas, since the thought of doing something that is less than perfect causes anxiety attacks. (This also may be true for overt perfectionists.) They may wait until the fear goes away before beginning or taking any steps forward, but of course it never does.

As a student I was average, and occasionally less than average. I never got As in high school or college. As a child with very bright and successful siblings, I made the decision that I couldn't do it as well as they could — that is, as perfectly — so why bother? I declared myself incapable and average, and settled into this pattern. I was very surprised when in graduate school (as a healthier person) I excelled without much effort at all.

Covert perfectionists may be capable of great things. But they have such fear of failure that they don't challenge themselves. Others may describe them as "laid back," but internally they still believe they should be doing things perfectly.

On occasion, covert perfectionists may lapse into depression with the slightest failure, exhibiting more outwardly their very high expectations of themselves. In the area of relationships, perfectionism in the way they respond to others may be a well-kept secret.

Linda described herself as a people pleaser. As a friend she believed that she should always be there, know instinctively when she was needed, call regularly, never forget a birthday or special occasion, never get angry or be selfish. Even when her friends didn't need anything, she worried that she was not doing enough.

The expectations she had of herself in relationships were so high that eventually Linda started avoiding her friends — not without guilt, of course. She interpreted this as, "They expect too much of me," and withdrew. Her perfectionism in her friendships led to a decision that being alone was better, since she didn't disappoint anyone.

Covert perfectionists may not look extremely neat. Yet they believe they are worthless because they are not neat. Their standards are so high that they cannot possibly be met, so they give up once again and resign themselves to being sloppy, overweight, uncoordinated and so on. If they were making a choice to have a more relaxed appearance because they liked it that way, this would be a very positive decision. The problem is in their fear of failure and resignation to the "fact" that "I can't do it."

Not everyone is a perfectionist. The real test is in the belief system and in the motivation behind the outward behavior. If you are truly exercising choice in that behavior, it is not perfectionism or any other compulsion. But I believe it is safe to say if you are reading this book you probably have some perfectionistic tendencies. For the remainder of this book, however, we will talk about "you" and "us" and "our problems."

2

Who Are
The Perfectionists?

Who are the perfectionists? It can be hard to tell. In fact it even may be difficult for you to know about yourself. In this chapter we'll look at some ways to find out.

Self-Test For Perfectionists

This list is a guide to help you determine the degree of perfectionism in yourself. Most people have a few positive responses, but if you check three or more you are experiencing greater stress than the average person.

☐ I place excessive demands on myself.
☐ Others would describe me as a perfectionist.
☐ I often obsess about the details of a task, even though it may not be important.

☐ I am annoyed when others don't act or behave as well as I do (e.g., be on time, keep order and so on).

☐ I am very organized in one or more areas of my life.

☐ I get very upset with myself if I make a mistake.

☐ I often have a mental list of things I "should be doing."

☐ I never seem to be doing enough.

☐ I tend to notice any error in myself or others before I notice the positive.

☐ I have an "all or nothing" philosophy: If I can't do it all, or do it well, why bother?

☐ I am devastated by criticism.

☐ I have difficulty making decisions.

Indicators Of Perfectionism

Yes, there are guideposts to point out perfectionist behavior. Most perfectionists will identify with a number of the following indicators of perfectionism.

Avoidance Of Stillness And Quiet

The negative self-talk we become so accustomed to makes it difficult for us to enjoy moments of peace. Some have described those critical voices as the "committee." They tell us we aren't doing enough, that we are stupid and on and on. When we stop our compulsive behavior we are haunted with unexplained feelings of guilt, shame, anger, hurt or fear.

As a college student I can recall studying in a student lounge, filled with conversation and smoke, while I played pinochle and listened to music. It was a joke among my friends that I would break the record for fewest hours spent in the library in a college career. I could not concentrate when it was quiet because the committee was in session!

Many of us use frenetic activity to distract us. We bustle around the house or office at a constant pace with the television or radio on to drown out our thoughts. Dan, for example, was 12 years old when he took on a job as a short-order cook in an extremely busy fast-food restaurant. He dedicated himself to becoming the best cook: "We used to serve 140 people in a half hour. I could remember eight or nine orders in my mind and then somebody would ask for a check and I would add it up in my head — including the tax — while I took care of what was cooking and someone was talking to me."

Dan, the child of two alcoholic parents, found great comfort and distraction in his work. But this method of avoiding pain only worked while he was busy. As soon as he would stop, the voices of inadequacy would begin. To quiet them Dan would smoke a joint on his break.

This need for intensity affects our choice of career — we choose a stressful and chaotic job over a slower-paced but more enjoyable job. It also causes us to overlook problems in our lives. We could solve or prevent them, but instead we tolerate bad situations and procrastinate on solutions.

Recovery requires slowing down the mental clatter so that feelings can come to the surface.

Placing Excessive Demands On Time And Energy, Feeling Like You Are Never Doing Enough

Perfectionists frequently set themselves up to fail with the fatal "To Do" list. They function as if someone were standing over them with a whip saying, "Do more, do more!"

On a typical Saturday, after working 40 or more hours in the week, Les would rise at 8:00 a.m. thinking he should have been up earlier. He would then look at his list and begin to add to it:

- Clean garage
- Take Mom to the mall
- Cut the grass
- Fix bathroom sink
- Take watch to be fixed
- Get Joan (wife) a birthday present
- Help Todd (brother) rotate tires
- Iron clothes

Around 3:30 p.m. Les would realize he had not played ball with his son or talked to his wife, and that he would not finish what he had planned for the day. Another day off had been blown. At this point he began to feel worthless and inadequate because he did not do enough. He felt very tired but he ignored it, since he had so much more to do.

When he walks around his home and yard, Les sees only what he has not yet done, and every project calls out to him. No matter what he does, it isn't enough. The list he created carries over to Sunday with a few more items added. Sadly he leaves himself no time for contact with himself or those he loves. He will get to it when he finishes the list . . .

Many perfectionists play victim to the clock, believing that if only there were more time, they would get it all done. The fact is *we never will.* The things we put off as "unimportant" are such items as intimacy, parenting, fun and exercise. We intend to get to these things but rarely do. We may even feel guilty and inadequate about not playing enough. The old tape plays on and on.

Ignoring our own bodies and our physical limitations prevents us from tuning in to what we really need and want. This leads to depression, illness and isolation from others.

Obsessing About The Details Of A Task, Overwhelming Ourselves With The Enormity Of It

The most anxiety-producing thing I have ever experienced is the anticipation of writing a book. Other people worry about the term paper that will be due at the end of the semester, the speech you are giving in five months, the house that needs remodeling, the new job you will be seeking next year, and on and on.

Perfectionists know that they must do the anticipated project perfectly, and they start to worry about it as early as possible. We act as if the entire project were in front of us at this moment, and we feel incapable of doing the whole thing right now. We are unable to break it down into manageable parts and may "catastrophize" it until it looks impossible.

Some people even have a physical response such as nausea, heart pounding, cold sweats or diarrhea at the mere thought of beginning.

As a result we tend to avoid anything that arouses anxiety, while waiting for the fear to go away. Candy shares her experience: "When I was younger I never attempted to do anything if there was a chance I might fail. Failure was not allowed in my home. If I had a challenge ahead of me, like a test, I would think about it with dread and terror months or weeks in advance. If there was a way to avoid it, I would. Often I would end up so scared I would put it off until the last minute and cram the night before an exam. I would still do well but I couldn't take credit for it. I quit college halfway through and never went back because of my perfectionism."

Many adults spend years wanting to go to college, but put it off while they wait to feel confident about it. The belief that they have to do it perfectly is compounded by the obsession with details. The result is procrastination and indecision.

Those who do achieve their desired goal drive themselves crazy in the process. They tend to over-prepare, compare themselves to others who have done similar work, redo until they are totally satisfied and worry every step of the way.

Being Frustrated With And Criticizing The Imperfections Of Others

The internal critical voice we use on ourselves is also projected onto others. We apply the same high standards of performance we cannot meet to those with whom we relate. Perfectionists may feel angry and frustrated with everyday human error, such as lateness, sloppy housekeeping, poor manners, word usage or poor work performance, but they are often criticizing qualities they themselves have.

Melanie says, "I really can't stand to hear a grammatical error — at least when I'm listening to a lecture or presentation (sometimes even in casual conversation), and I get terribly distracted when reading if I see a mistake. In fact, I sometimes get angry at the writer; and if there are a number of errors I might even stop reading the item entirely!" It is no surprise to discover that Melanie had perfectionist parents, who also were critical and pointed out every error in anything she said or wrote.

Jean, a recovering co-dependent, was frequently told by friends and family that she seemed angry and impatient most of the time. Before she began treatment Jean was extremely difficult to work with. As a nursing supervisor she focused consistently on the mistakes of her employees. She believed that if she wanted something done right, she had to do it herself. Her performance evaluations pointed out her need to control and her lack of confidence in her staff.

Since Jean believed that she worked harder and better than everyone else, she could not accept this feedback. She blamed her supervisor for not understanding her difficult situation. She felt overworked and unappreciated.

At home Jean was very critical with her children. When looking at a school paper with her son, she would immediately see the flaw and comment on it. She found herself treating them in much the way she had been treated as a child and became frightened by it.

In co-dependency treatment Jean discovered that the way she viewed others was a reflection of what she felt about herself. In a way this focus on the flaws of others allowed her to avoid her own. In reality she believed that she was worthless and should be perfect. This belief had to change before she could be more accepting of others.

This characteristic of being critical of others can be extremely damaging to people close to the perfectionist. It is expecially difficult in roles where we exercise authority, such as a parent or supervisor.

Practicing Rigid, Purposeless Rituals In The Name Of Organization, Structure, Cleanliness Or Believing It Is The Right Way

In his work life Tom made extensive lists of every task. He drew columns and lines on each page in a special notebook, putting little boxes before each line to be checked off later. It took him up to an hour each day to do this.

Janet was married to an alcoholic. Although she described her life as totally unmanageable, her house was always in perfect order. She vacuumed every room every day until her therapy group finally told her she didn't need to do this. Giving it up was not easy. Doing so meant having idle time to feel her pain.

One perfectionist described her father's orderliness at home: "My dad was a genius, the vice president of a major corporation. When he was at home, he would relax by working in his workshop. His tools were always arranged largest to smallest — screw drivers, hammers, socket wrenches, all arranged the same way. He built cabinets that held perfectly arranged sets of drill bits and special racks that held perfectly arranged grades of sandpaper. A special closet held labeled and numbered cans of paint, varnish and wood stain. The closet door held an array of perfectly displayed paint brushes from the tiniest camel hair to a 5-inch-wide brush. These brushes were also arranged according to the brush composition and the type of job they were purchased for. When the firemen came for their yearly inspection, they were always amazed at our basement. Nothing was ever out of place. When my dad died, I realized that I never really knew him."

Other examples of perfectionistic rituals include:

- Ironing underwear.
- Waxing the car weekly (not because it needs it, but because you are supposed to).
- Washing dresser drawers twice a year.
- Sending thank you notes for cards received on your birthday.
- Planning in detail any excursion from home, even shopping, and declining any invitation with short notice.
- Spending hours in organizing activities and only minutes in doing them.

None of these things is a problem in and of itself. In fact others may even admire a person who has such discipline. The difficulty begins when things like intimacy, relaxation and children take a back seat to the need for order, and when the organizing and cleaning have become medicators for emotional pain.

Fearing Failure And Feeling Inadequate, Guilty And Sometimes Shameful When Our Humanness Shows

Perfectionists operate from the belief that they should be perfect and then beat themselves whenever they fall short. This is often quite extreme in one area of life but hardly visible in another.

Although Ed appeared to be a liberal, laid-back sort of guy, he judged himself harshly in his interpersonal relationships. He had the expectation that he should never cause displeasure for those he loved. In therapy Ed described this frequent scenario: after an encounter with a family member or friend, he would find himself mentally reviewing everything he said and did, looking for the flaw in his behavior. He would begin to feel guilty for some slight comment he *may* have made which he thought *might* have been insensitive or hurtful.

All of this would take place in his head, with no evidence that the other person was actually upset or hurt. Ed's feelings of guilt would grow until they were no longer about his behavior but were a reflection of his worth as a person. This stronger, deeper pain is called shame.

At this point Ed would feel bad, worthless and unlovable. After hours or days of emotional turmoil, Ed would then call the person he believed he had offended and apologize. The supposed victim of his error usually did not recall the event and was not offended in the least. Once forgiven, Ed would feel better, vowing never to make such an error again — which is, unfortunately, humanly impossible.

Virtually every perfectionist with whom I have had contact feels paralyzed by fear of failure. Amy wrote, "I hate to fail. It isn't that I made a mistake or that something didn't work out, it's that *I* am a failure. Even if I've never done something before, if I fail, I'm devastated. I can beat myself up for months because of a failure. Either that, or I convince myself that it doesn't matter, and I have a hard time taking a risk and trying that activity or similar activities again."

Another commented, "I had a job once, a job I really didn't like, and I was told by my supervisor that this job was not working out for me. I burst into tears in my boss's office, sobbing, 'I've never failed at anything before.' Rather than look at how I could improve or make changes and rationally come to a decision about the job, I quit immediately. For weeks after that I couldn't sleep without having dreams about failing. This issue finally brought me to therapy."

The perfectionist's self-esteem is fragile and totally based on performance. The person is thus destroyed by the discovery of an actual or perceived flaw.

Competing Mentally Or Behaviorally In Any Endeavor

We all know someone who appears to be extremely competitive in many areas of their lives. They often are seen as determined, ambitious, energetic or even driven to win. In some areas of his or her life the overt perfectionist may feel the need to be the best and yet never feel satisfied with the outcome. Upon winning, a little voice says something like:

- "He was tired today, that's why I won at racquetball."
- "I only got an A because we weren't tested on anything I didn't study."
- "I got the promotion, but I really don't deserve it. If the boss finds out who I really am, I'll be fired."
- "I may be very successful, but what about so and so who does so much more, makes more money, is smarter?"
- "My wife says I'm a great lover but she's probably faking."
- "What have I done lately?"

The point is that even those who look like they are the best struggle with those negative voices. They have the notion that in order to feel OK they must be better than others. Jan for example, was talented at most everything she attempted. But, she confided, "I find it hard now to see myself as 'OK' and 'acceptable' as I am. I feel I must earn acceptance from others, by doing all things *well.* In order to feel good about myself and cover up the shame and guilt that I carry, I have become very preoccupied with my tennis playing — an hour and a half each morning. I get very upset at myself when I fail to execute a shot that would be a winner, that I have made before but failed to do this particular time. I think I must be carrying a message inside that says, "I'm sorry I can't be what you want me to be."

The covert perfectionist also is competitive, but it's more internal. They may expend much energy observing the successes of others, believing they should have the same gifts, abilities and accomplishments. They may jokingly comment on how noncompetitive they are, while internally they are critically evaluating themselves in comparison to others.

One covert perfectionist had this to say about the mental anguish of believing you should be the best: "In my academic work I spent years simply avoiding anything at which I thought I might not be outstanding. This meant that I sold myself short and deprived myself of years of learning and experiences that might have been exciting, rather than risk being mediocre." Although she graduated eighth in a class of 360, she still believed it was not good enough.

Perfectionists also may become extremely uncomfortable when a spouse, co-worker or friend experiences success. They feel inadequate and "less than" the other person.

Having An All-Or-Nothing Philosophy, Believing In Absolutes

The perfectionist uses terms (mentally, if not verbally), such as right-wrong, always-never, good-bad, all-or-nothing, should, must and so on. These terms reflect the belief that there actually is a correct way to think and be. The truth, of course, is all relative — determined by an individual at a particular time and place and given a specific set of circumstances. People and their views are as numerous as the stars in the sky. Nonetheless perfectionists believe they must find the right way, perform that way and convince others to do the same.

Some examples of such extreme thinking include:

- People should always be on time.
- In an argument it is essential to determine who is right and who is wrong. You must convince the other person that your way is right and should not give up until they agree.

- An activity shared with someone else is either good or bad. We should agree on our perceptions of that experience.
- There is a proper way to drive a car, talk to others, dress, work and so on. If you or I do not perform this way we are at fault.

Perfectionist students may silently harbor the belief that they should know everything there is to know about a particular subject before taking a test or submitting a paper. I remember thinking that I should have read cover to cover every book on alcoholism before writing my master's thesis. Even though I received an A, I secretly believed that my paper wasn't as good as it should have been.

When confronted with this thinking pattern, most perfectionists would acknowledge that it is neither realistic nor possible to be perfectly correct or thorough. But because we operate from low self-worth and emotional pain we may believe that others are capable and we are just not as good. This is a compulsive — not rational — pattern of thinking. One possible payoff is that since we cannot do it perfectly, we might as well not do it at all.

Struggling With Spirituality, Feeling Unworthy And Judged

The term "spirituality" implies an emotional, intimate connection with both something greater than ourselves and with our own internal spirit. The "something greater" may mean God and religion; but it also may mean a very strong belief in any group or concept, such as love, fellowship and so on. It suggests a need or dependence on God or others for something we do not have alone.

The inner connection with one's spirit often is referred to as the inner child: a strong sense of who we are and who we were meant to be. This connection is without judgment and is one of love and appreciation for oneself. Spirituality and perfectionism are contradictory terms because the perfectionist is trying to be God.

Perfectionists operate from the belief that they will be accepted by God, self or others only after they achieve a perfect state. Any attempt at spiritual connection will be focused on performance of ritual, duty and approval-seeking rather than from an instinctive, intuitive desire to reach beyond human limitation to something more meaningful.

Lorraine, now in recovery for her co-dependency, described how her strict religious upbringing coupled with her perfectionism made it very difficult for her to rely on a loving God. "My religious training as a child convinced me that I had to be perfect. After all, God was keeping track of all my actions. I found it particularly disconcerting when I had to go to confession. I feared for lack of acceptance from God so I usually did a lot of rationalizing to keep from having to confess a mortal sin. Because of my understanding of the last judgment I expected to find myself sitting in a giant movie theater with all the world watching, as all my transgressions passed across the screen. It never occurred to me that God might be more interested in the good things I had done rather than the bad."

Our experience living in a dysfunctional family and our difficulties with the most significant authority figures in our lives — our parents — alter our perceptions of a Higher Power and make it impossible to accept that anyone could or would love us unconditionally. Spiritual recovery will be easier if we face our fears and anger with parents in a treatment setting before we attempt total surrender to a Higher Power.

Attempting To Be The Perfect Recovering Person

Regardless of the impetus for entering into the recovery process — chemical dependency, compulsive overeating, co-dependency — the perfectionist, once motivated, will dive in with both feet (see Chapter 5 for more on treatment). The shame intrinsic to the illness will create a need to get well fast and to do it right.

Sam was the child of two alcoholic parents and chemically dependent himself. When he began his recovery, he did everything he was asked to do by members of his AA group. Before too long he had a sponsor, was working the Steps exactly as he had been directed and began to do some service work as well. Sam went to meetings seven days a week, meditated daily and even read numerous books on the subject. After eight months he relapsed. Why?

Like Sam, many perfectionists in recovery change their behavior and language long before they actually begin the internal change required for lasting recovery. They have spent a lifetime avoiding their shame by doing and performing. In recovery they quickly catch on to the expectations of their group, therapist and peers. They know how to look good. Unfortunately, their feelings may not change and will inevitably sabotage all the effort to recover perfectly.

Here are some warning signs of perfectionism in recovery:

- Becoming overly zealous in learning all there is to know about your illness, family and so on. You may find yourself looking feverishly for one simple explanation for everything that is wrong with you. You will never learn it all. Experts will never know it all either!
- Trying too hard to be the perfect 12-Step group member. Perhaps you feel you don't talk well enough or often enough, or maybe you talk too much at meetings. You may even find yourself reorganizing the meeting format, literature or coffee setup. Service is important; but perfectionists may begin to turn a support system into a problem.
- Maintaining, even in a support group or therapy group, a Looking Good image. Learning the words of recovery, the slogans and jargon, and becoming too well, too fast only serves to convince others that you don't need anything. Before you know it, you are either surrounded with others who need you or you're alone and unapproachable.
- Comparing yourself to others who began before you or even with you, and actually competing in recovery. Each of us works at our own pace, and the time it will take depends on our history along with many other factors.
- Expecting perfect consistency from yourself in recovery. Believing that you should never slide back into old ways

of acting, lose control of yourself, caretake, overwork and
so on. All of us do these things some of the time.
- Minimizing progress while making lists of your defects
that need work. On any day we can choose to look at
how far we've come or how far we need to go. Perfectionists in recovery need to focus on the positive.
- Attempting to perfect and fix one's family so that it too
will look good. Our energy needs to be spent on changing ourselves and being supportive of others as they
make their own choices.
- Parenting with perfection. Moving too quickly, out of
shame, to fix our children and repair all damage done
in the past. Reading books, reciting affirmations and
pushing them to share feelings does not work as well as
just changing yourself and modeling health.
- Seeking perfection as a long-term goal in recovery. Some
of us continue to harbor the belief that if we do this
right, we will be free of painful emotions, character
defects and our history forever. Even if this is at an
unconscious level, it will frustrate us as we struggle to
accept ourselves as we are, one day at a time.

Perfectionism in the recovery process is inevitable if this has
been a lifetime pattern. After all, we bring ourselves with us!

3

The Price
Of Perfection

When I speak publicly about perfectionism, my audiences are quite receptive and even entertained by the subject. The humor with which we approach the topic is a reflection of our minimization of its severity. We — myself included — just don't take it that seriously. Our families and friends may tease us about it, we may feel a bit irritated with it, but is it really all that big a deal?

The negative side of the story is the price we pay for our perfectionism. I have drawn from the shared experiences of those I surveyed and interviewed, as well as comments of workshop participants.

The Survey

It was not unusual for people to critique the survey while they completed it. Most were very uncomfortable with simply responding yes or no and wrote many explanations for their answers. Some even attached letters, giving me input on how I might have done it better. (Yes, I used some of their suggestions!)

Survey Results

I surveyed 126 people — 70 percent women and 30 percent men. I believe men suffer from perfectionism every bit as often as women, but my source of participants was primarily the human service network which is heavily weighted with women. Of the respondents, 33 percent were recovering from chemical dependence.

Regarding family history, 94 percent reported a moderate to severely dysfunctional family of origin; 46 percent reported a perfectionist parent and 45 percent (with some overlap) reported a workaholic parent. It is very common to have both of these problems at the same time because they are the popular, acceptable addictions in our society.

Of those surveyed, 50 percent were firstborn children.

Men and women were slightly different in describing their own perfectionism. All of the men and 47 percent of the women listed work as the number one area affected. The remaining women listed as number one in this order: parenting, physical appearance, household responsibilities, relationships, sex and health.

The majority of those surveyed felt that others were moderately to severely affected by their perfectionism. They listed as problematic in relationships in this order: control issues, lack of intimacy and shared feelings, gaps in levels of recovery between partners, communication.

Health problems were listed for 95 percent. Some described very serious stress-related conditions, others reported chronic but less severe problems. Asked to list their most serious health problem, participants stated as number one in this order: headaches and sleep disturbance, digestive problems and back pain, overeating, sexual dysfunction and chest pain.

Intrapersonal difficulties with procrastination, decision-making, depression and even suicidal thoughts were listed by the majority of those surveyed. The area of decision-making was listed as problematic for 70 percent. When asked the question, do you have difficulty making decisions? Yes or No? Several answered "Sometimes."

Upon making a decision, 75 percent struggle with doubts afterward; 58 percent reported occasional suicidal thoughts and a few had attempted suicide in the past. This figure is not unlike any report about co-dependents, who frequently reach such depths of depression that they see suicide as the only way out.

Asked how often they actually achieve perfection, 10 percent answered "frequently"; 50 percent responded "once in a while"; and 40 percent said "never." This indicates that the majority of perfectionists have some success — or believe they do — in the pursuit of perfection.

The Consequences Of Perfectionism

As our perfectionistic compulsion progresses, each area of our lives seems to show some deterioration. Those most often reported as damaged are work, parenting and being parented by a perfectionist, health, body image and relationships.

Perfectionism at Work

In my own life, work was the area most affected by my perfectionism. I began working in the addiction field 16 years ago in a street detox, a job only a co-dependent could love. I took my self-worth from the job and needed it to go well for me to be OK. Unlike my personal life, which seemed to be out of my hands, I felt that I had some control in the workplace even though I was a very low-paid and unappreciated counselor.

One thing I've always known how to do is work hard. Even when I was a waitress in college I had to be the best waitress. In the detox unit I felt responsible for everything — from the wino's clothes being washed, to the quality of the food, to the program design, to whether or not a person stayed sober. My personal life was totally unmanageable at the time, but I knew what I was doing when I went to work.

Ironically I was only being paid for one-third of the duties
I assumed were mine. I could not understand why I was not
appreciated or compensated for what I did. In hindsight I
realized that I must have been impossible to deal with as an
employee. I was extremely critical of anyone who did not do
things as well as I, or who did not totally agree with me. I was
a workaholic who had a hard time understanding people who
simply worked to earn money!

Eventually I was fired for attacking my boss and telling him
what to do. I may even have been right. But that doesn't
matter much when you're unemployed, does it?

Following that experience I decided that I knew how it
should be done and began to develop programs of my own.
I did some fine work but I did most of it alone for a few years
in the belief that no one could do it as well as I. At one point
I had 60 outpatient clients, did four therapy groups per week
and was director. People admired my ability to do everything
and they let me. Superwoman flies again!

Fortunately I began recovery. Today I have learned to operate as part of a team and to delegate and seek help from
others. I love it this way, but it does require that I feel and tend
to my personal life. Perfectionism and workaholism were
handy tools to help me avoid my personal life. They don't
work for me anymore.

Schoolwork

The word *work* means many things depending on our life-
style or stage of development. As children, and often in adult
life as well, perfectionists exercise their compulsive behavior
in school. Sandy remembers vividly trying to be Little Miss
Perfect: "I was nine years old and I was teaching the Palmer
method in a Catholic school — I was put in charge when the
nun would leave the room. I couldn't have any friends because
I was a miniature teacher." Sandy needed the praise and even
enjoyed it, but was aware of the isolation that resulted from
being too good.

For many, achievement in school was the only way to gain
attention and approval from parents. One young man discov-

ered the unpredictability of this kind of approval: "My father — who had quite literally ignored me for the first 16 years of my life — finally noticed me when I got nearly perfect S.A.T. scores. Suddenly this man who never talked to me about school, realized that I might get into any college and spent all his time that summer driving me to every Ivy League school on the East Coast. It was very uncomfortable for me."

Even if school memories are very painful, these same patterns often continue into the workplace. Mary says, "As a child I always wanted to do what was asked of me. At school I was quiet, sat at my desk with hands folded in front of me. I was fearful of authority figures and at the same time wanted their approval. I remember my penmanship class and how very careful I was to be as perfect and neat as possible. In my early teen years my notebooks were orderly and neat, my drawings of lab specimens nicely labeled using colors and so on.

"As an adult this pattern continued. I sought out more work and responsibility and it always felt like it was never enough. My papers and writings were neat and my work areas clean and organized. I was once told that I worked so rapidly that I appeared to be mechanically producing great volumes of work and not thinking about what I was doing. I always had the sense that if I learned enough things, I would be worthy to be alive."

Household Responsibilities

Household responsibilities can become ghosts that haunt day and night, saying, "Remember me? I'm the dirty closet you haven't cleaned in two years!" When a person is workaholic, home cannot be perfect — but there still may be the expectation that it should be.

Perfectionists look at homes in magazines and expect theirs to be the same. Sandy, a successful businesswoman, says, "When I saw a picture in a magazine, that's how my home was supposed to be. It may have taken a photographer five days to arrange that shot for one picture but I would think, 'Oh, so that's the way a house is supposed to look.' And when you open the door, you're supposed to look like a movie star opening the door on this perfect house, the perfect car and the fresh flowers are right there, perfectly arranged."

Many women seem to deal with their shame through tidying and cleaning their homes. At the same time, if they are unable to do it, some resort to all or nothing and live in total disorder. "If I can't do it perfectly, why bother?" She may not allow anyone into the house because she is so ashamed, even restricting children from having friends over. Covert perfectionists may have a messy house due to the hectic life they lead; but they secretly believe that until it is perfect they will never be OK.

Whenever a perfectionist tries to relax there is always the haunting voice of the *house* saying, "Wash the curtains, clean the garage and the attic, shampoo the rugs!" The house becomes a nagging person instead of a place of safety and shelter. It is the voice of the perfectionist that makes this happen, not that of the structure in which we reside.

It is possible for the critical part of the perfectionist to also expect these things of a spouse or roommate. Larry grew up with a mother who kept a perfect house and he married a woman who was totally unorganized and very sloppy. He spent a great deal of this time noticing and commenting on things that were not done in the home. Larry and his wife had many arguments about the right way to clean; they rarely discussed the problems of their relationship. The order or disorder of the house was more important than the disorder in their marriage.

Fear Of Criticism In The Workplace

Fear of criticism is the fear that others will find out what frauds we are and abandon us. This is a constant nagging concern for the perfectionist in the workplace and in any relationship. Erin, for example, was an administrative assistant in a law office, a job she performed flawlessly and alone. Her only difficulty came with her tendency to make decisions independently without checking it out with her co-workers. She spent much of her energy trying to avoid criticism and had to avoid people in the process.

When Erin was evaluated, her boss had many positive comments about the quantity of work she performed and her strong personal commitment. But he also commented on her isolation. Characteristically Erin distorted her feedback and heard only one thing: "You make bad decisions, people don't like you." She did not hear the rest of her evaluation. At first Erin felt embarrassed, then ashamed and finally — an hour later — she was furious. She believed she was unappreciated and should quit.

Erin expected her boss to catch her making a mistake and fire her. She worried constantly about not doing enough or missing something. Whenever the boss asked to see her, she cringed, knowing this was the end. It never occurred to her that admitting she did not know something and asking for help would probably greatly enhance her performance and keep her employed.

Erin had been through this before in other jobs. Her solution was to leave before they found out any more about her and start fresh in another workplace. She blamed each employer for expecting too much and not thanking her enough.

Can't Enjoy Success

Perfectionists often have great success at what they do in terms of status achieved or even financial gains. They start out believing that the reason they don't feel OK is that they have not done enough. Once they arrive at that identified place (certain salary, promotion, graduation, being published) they expect to feel better. And so they work harder, better and longer than anyone else. Once they meet the initial goal they have identified a new level that they must achieve in order to be OK.

When I wrote my first book, a dream I had held for many years, I expected to feel elated and satisfied with my accomplishment. But instead I felt very detached from what I had done. I could not own it. I read the words and could not imagine that they came from me. In order to appreciate and thank myself for doing it I asked friends to help me and even threw a party for myself. It helped a lot until time passed.

Then I noticed that my peers had written more than one book, in fact more than two, and I began to discount what I had done. In writing my second book I worked on enjoying the process instead of striving for the goal.

A very large part of our lives is spent in the workplace. In recovery we need to focus a lot of effort on achieving some balance in this area.

Perfectionists And Parenting

The Child Of A Perfectionist

Being the child of a perfectionist is extremely difficult. Judy had two perfectionistic parents: "The problem with having perfectionist parents is that they are very inconsistent in their demands. I never knew what I was supposed to be perfect at and what didn't matter. The perfectionism in my family is selective and therefore very confusing. If my parents wanted to do something (or wanted it done), they expected it to be perfect. If it was a task that they didn't care about, it didn't matter how it was done.

"Often they gave me the tasks that they didn't like, and expected perfection from me on the tasks that they would do carelessly. They were never satisfied with anything I did. It wasn't good enough."

The fact is that perfectionism does not make sense. From the child's perspective it is abusive and unreasonable. Children know instinctively that it is impossible to be perfect. Developmentally it may be beyond their reach. Judy has this painful memory: "I remember my father asking me to do something for him, like go get a tool. He would very abruptly give me an order, expecting that I had all the information he did. I did not know one tool from another, even if he had told me before. When I would come back with the wrong one, he'd call me stupid and scream at me. Then I couldn't think at all and I'd make more mistakes. The more he expected of me, the less I could perform. The anxiety about making a mistake started to make me sick. I'd get stomachaches and headaches all the time."

If a child were disciplined enough to clean a bedroom to the point of perfect order, the child would probably be abused and emotionally disturbed. It is not normal for children to do dishes, make beds, wash the car, vacuum or dust like an adult. It is also useless to suggest to children that there actually is a "right" way to do everything. Soon they grow up, go out into the world and find out that there are thousands of "right" ways.

They haven't learned to think for themselves so they keep looking for the rule book to guide them. One client, role playing in group therapy, faced her "family" in a childlike manner and asked plaintively, "Just tell me what I'm supposed to do, and I'll do it!" The fact is they had been telling her for years but she kept waiting for the approval, which never came. She was a very good person, able and willing to do what was expected; but the rules kept changing and the rewards never came. She was lost.

"Perfect" Parenting

Often the children of perfectionists grow up without realizing there was anything wrong and parent their children the way they were parented. Even those who hate what was done to them tend to repeat the family pattern. It also is common for adults who grew up in chaos to decide to do the opposite with their own children. These perfectionists go to the extreme called perfect parenting. A few people I interviewed were so determined to be perfect parents that they did not have children at all. Since they also have difficulty making decisions many put off having children out of fear, until it was too late.

The Looking Good family, a focus of my book *Grandchildren of Alcoholics,* is an apt description of the dynamics of a family with a perfectionistic parent or parents. Often the motivation for trying so hard to do it right is to overcome a painful family history and to show their parents and the world how it should be done. They do this with the hope that the parents will feel good about them if it turns out well, and also serves to make external order out of internal disorder.

Parenting in this family is done with a great deal of control. The ability to control family dynamics, children or even life events is a myth at best and is doomed to fail. Ironically the perfectionist parent, when feeling out of control, uses old familiar methods and tries to control more in order to feel better. Examples of such control might include:

- Rigid order: Everything has a proper place (or at least the belongings of the perfectionist do!).
- Cleanliness is more important than life, relationships, fun, being a child: "Don't get dirty, work first, play later."
- Plan, plan, plan but do very little. Everything must be planned ahead and is therefore too much trouble. Without proper notice and planning, a mistake may be made. So the family does very little, and certainly nothing spontaneous.
- What will the neighbors think? Children must look, talk and act perfectly or Mom and Dad will look bad. The preacher's kids for example, need to present a proper image, no matter how it feels, so that others will think well of Dad.
- Fun becomes work. Playing — at sports, music and so on — must be done as well as possible. Children must always strive to do it better, longer, faster than before.
- Strive for excellence. Always do your best, especially at school where others will notice. The message is that you, the child, should accomplish what your parents couldn't — or least do as well as they did.
- Don't get sick. Some families obsess about health issues, dressing right for the weather, taking children's temperature frequently, keeping children away from friends who may have germs, force feeding vegetables and vitamins.
- "Eat right so that I'll feel like a good mother." The parent decides if and when you are hungry. Older children must ask if they can have a drink or a cookie. Food intake is controlled and dictated.

Perfect Parents rely on these external controls to try to gain a sense of internal comfort. They do not intend to abuse their

their children. In fact, they believe they are creating the best possible environment to prepare children for the world. The fault is often in trying too hard and having too much.

Family togetherness becomes enmeshment. There is no space, privacy or individual identity. A desire to be close to one's children leads to crossing of healthy boundaries. Wanting to do good things with children, whether sports, travel or other positive activities, becomes imposed and abusive.

Children raised in this rigid Looking Good atmosphere are so smothered and controlled they often have no choice but to rebel. Being defiant, sick or sloppy, getting poor grades or just plain refusing to cooperate are almost necessary tools for survival. Some children grow up to be perfectionists and just keep trying.

One ACoA with a perfectionistic mother wrote, "At 6 a.m. I would practice piano for a half hour and my sister would then do the same. I believed that if only I was good enough, Dad would stop drinking and Mom would be OK. If I complained, Mom would cry. So I just tried to be the best little girl I could be. My younger sister didn't comply the way I did. She left as soon as she could and, ironically, they liked her better."

Diana is a perfectionist mother who had been raised in an abusive home. She spoke of the exhaustion of trying to be all things to her children and failing miserably because she had no limits. She believed that if only she could get order and perfection with her children, her failing marriage and her low self-esteem would heal.

In recovery we find that parenting is not about what we tell our children to do or be, but about who we are.

Health And Body Image

Messages about the need for physical perfection are all around us:

- Oil of Olay will help you stay young.
- Jane Fonda can turn a 40-year-old woman into a perfect physical specimen.
- Dial soap will give you self-esteem.

- Grecian Formula takes years off your appearance.
- Special formulas for hair loss tell us that it's bad to allow
  nature to run its course.

Recent health crazes include being constantly aware of your
cholesterol level, blood pressure, fat intake, environmental
hazards and on and on. It all seems pretty positive and harmless until it is put in the hands of a perfectionist. We respond
with alarming compulsion to the shoulds placed on us by
advertising, society, and family and friends.

Our desire to fix up our outsides to soothe our insides,
combined with our competitive nature (we should look as
good as any friend who is in shape or the person in the ad)
push us to have the perfect body and to be in perfect health.
Of course we don't achieve it; and even those who come
close are never good enough, striving for more and more.

The problem is not in what we are doing or not doing, but
in our reasons for trying and our belief that we should have
it all. I have encountered several different but equally dysfunctional expressions of this pattern:

1. *Compulsive dieter/exercisers* must do aerobics three
   times per week, jog for one hour every day and be
   vegetarian. Painful feelings, shame and inadequacy surface as soon as they stop, which is often due to injury.
   The same people may flip over and doing nothing in the
   belief that if you can't do it right, it's not worth anything.
2. *Physical disasters* believe in perfection but know that
   they will never do it well enough and they might as well
   enjoy. They smoke, they're overweight, they hate exercise
   and anyone who does it. They are passive participants in
   life, planning to get to it sometime. Their feelings of
   inadequacy show on the outside. The belief system for
   #1 and #2 are identical.
3. *Health nuts* become experts in nutrition and homeo-
   pathic remedies, medicating any minor symptom, perhaps looking for specific emotions linked to specific
   physical symptoms. (A sore throat means you need to
   say something you're not saying.) They believe that they

should be in full control of their physical state at all times. A lovely idea, but hardly possible.

4. *Fatalists* say, "What's the use? I'm going to die anyway, the whole world is full of deadly diseases, an accident could kill me in a minute, so I might as well live it up!" These people may abuse themselves while waiting for the right conditions or the right relationship to change them. They are victims of the terrible world we live in. They could switch to #3 overnight!

5. *Physical appearance perfectionists* use every method known to our society to avoid aging, bulges, sagging, graying and so on. Plastic surgery is an option for those who can afford it, to be someone other than who they are. Makeup now can be custom designed. It is all based on the belief that others will love me and I will love myself if I can just get it right.

6. *Laid-back liberals* give up. Women let their underarm hair grow, believe that body odor is sexy, wear no make-up and scoff at women who wear uncomfortable clothes to be stylish. She may even outwardly criticize those sexist women! The outward expression is that, "I don't care what anyone thinks of me." The male is the same — not caring what he looks like. The inner belief is that "No one will ever accept me anyway, so I'll push them away first and not be hurt."

This list can be quite disturbing, since we all fit somewhere at one time or another. I've been into #3 in the last few years, and recognize that I secretly harbor the belief that if I get well enough inside, I won't have any illness outside. The problem really lies with the extreme rigid, perfectionistic, all-or-nothing thinking we carry on in our minds. Few of the behaviors mentioned are damaging, and some are very good. But when we are reacting rather than choosing, we are acting out of dysfunction. The tendency of the perfectionist is to flip from one extreme to the other, all in an effort to avoid painful feelings, particularly shame.

If we focus recovery on who we are *at this moment* rather than on who we should be, working on self-acceptance more than self-improvement, our outsides will start to show results. You'll find it easier to take good care of yourself when you've reached the decision that you truly are OK as you are right now.

"Perfect" Relationships

If you have seen only dysfunction in family relationships, you probably look at television families, at the neighbors, at friends, and assume that there really are perfect relationships. Well, I'm here to tell you that there are no perfect relationships. This makes sense when you realize that all relationships are made up of imperfect human beings who are frequently operating in opposing directions. (There are, however, some very healthy relationships, which we will explore in chapter 6.)

Perfectionists do not consider their relationships to be gravely affected, since most of their compulsivity is expressed around work. That in itself is a relationship problem. It takes time, commitment and dedication to maintain a relationship. Workaholics and perfectionists are stretched to the limit and have little time and energy to devote to a relationship.

How does perfectionism affect our relationships? The participants in my survey said that the areas of greatest difficulty for them were control issues, lack of intimacy and shared feelings, gaps in levels of emotional growth or recovery and communication.

The Need For Control

People who come from dysfunctional families often believe that control means safety. Being in control means having a predictable life where nothing happens that you can't handle; where your spouse or lover thinks like you, does things the way you do them, meets your needs (without being asked), expresses feelings (but only the ones you want to hear) and so on. Of course when we are asked to perform this way ourselves we know how impossible it is.

Control, like perfection, is an illusion. The few moments when you think you have it are probably just because the people in your life are letting you believe it for a while, so you'll stop trying to achieve it. It is an act of fear to attempt to overpower others, dictating or even just obsessing about how they should live, feel, act, talk, dress and so on. It serves to alienate others, causing them to fake it around you rather than be genuinely themselves. When you attempt to control another you are indirectly saying, "You aren't good enough the way you are. I can't trust you to make good judgments or to not hurt me. People will think badly of me if you aren't just right."

Those statements reflect what it feels like to be on the receiving end of control. Many perfectionists were raised with those voices and unintentionally play back old tapes in relationships.

There are moments in our lives — in a crisis situation, for example — when it is wise to take control. This is a choice. Dysfunctional control is not by choice. It is an attempt to gain safety by altering the outside world, including a primary relationship, to fit our needs. Since true feelings of safety come from within, this method does not work and often serves to destroy the relationship. Controlling people are also subject to being controlled because they are not tending to themselves and don't know who they are.

Lack Of Intimacy And Shared Feelings

We learn intimacy and expression of feelings from our parents. Adults from dysfunctional families don't have a clue about how to do it either. Perfectionism only compounds the problem further. Perfectionists, if they attend to their primary relationship at all, put a great deal of effort into the doing and little effort into being and feeling.

In friendships, for example, perfectionists may believe that "If I were a good friend, I would . . .

- Always remember your birthday, send a card and take you out to dinner."
- Know instinctively when you need something and provide it."
- Say thank you and return the favor whenever you do something for me."

- Like your spouse and children and enjoy them as much as you do."
- Talk to you on the phone at least twice a week and whenever you need to talk, no matter what I'm doing."

Granted, these sound a bit extreme. But perfectionists often harbor these secret notions and feel inadequate if they do not honor them.

In a primary relationship the perfectionist feels:
"If I am a good husband, wife, lover I will always . . .

- Have sex whenever you want, even if I'm tired."
- Listen to you talk about work for as long as you need."
- Understand when you don't have the energy to parent, help around the house, talk."
- Respect your need for space, even when I need you."

All of the above are focused on doing the right things to bring about the desired closeness in a relationship. We often pick up these ideas from reading books or watching TV, or maybe these are really what we expect others to do for us. They are very nice but none have anything to do with intimacy.

Even if many of these things were lacking, the relationship could still be intimate and healthy. Intimacy has to do with an emotional connection between two adults. Chapter 4 will address the ingredients more specifically.

Perfectionism in relating is a deterrent to intimacy. Intimacy requires that we let go, with no idea of the outcome. The active perfectionist cannot do this.

Gaps In Levels Of Emotional Growth And Recovery

When a co-dependent begins recovery and personal change, it is often with the hope that it will change others. After all, that's what co-dependency is. It can be very disappointing to find out that a spouse or lover is not interested in joining you on your journey and in fact may be going in a different direction. The difficulty comes when you become aware of the loneliness of recovery and understand that no one can join you in your struggles and feelings. Although we may feel supported by others, we are truly alone within ourselves, and maybe even alone in our primary relationship.

Making changes as significant as those in co-dependent recovery means letting go of what we think we are going to get and accomplish with the work we are doing. It may or may not be in the plan for us to continue the relationship we are in. Once self-esteem starts to rise many people vow never to be abused again, which makes the decision to back out of an abusive relationship much easier. For the majority, however, it is not that straightforward.

Over time you may become aware that you don't know the person you live with, or that the "you" who made that choice was not real, but a hurting soul looking for comfort from another hurting soul. With a lot of effort it is possible for a couple to meet again and start over as if they had just met. It will be just as difficult to end this relationship and start over with someone new. We bring ourselves and our history with us, and we repeat destructive patterns many times before we truly change.

Perfectionists often want easy solutions they can think through and implement. This is not an easily resolved area. As you change it is important to focus on yourself, trusting that you will be OK no matter what. That may even relieve some of that pressure to control and may improve things somewhat. Spouses, friends and children each need to make their own choices about recovery and cannot be forced into it because we think it's a good idea. This is an area where less is better. The less we do to force solutions, the quicker and easier they will come.

Communication

Many overt perfectionists believe there is a right way to communicate. Once again, however, they may be more concerned with how they give the message than with the message they are giving. It is true that we say more with our body language than with our words. We can be speaking perfectly, calmly and succinctly, yet be expressing rage toward the person we are talking to. It is very common for a talented linguist to be matched up with an emotionally expressive partner.

The perfectionist may out-talk the emotional person, using reason, logic and fancy words. This leaves the partner feeling abused and impotent but with no recourse, since the argument was so sound. Perfect word usage and logic do not constitute healthy communication. Problems develop when we try to hide our fears and other feelings behind our words. These attitudes and behaviors may be present when a perfectionist attempts to communicate safely:

1. Someone is right and someone is wrong. I must convince you that I am right and why, until you concede or feel foolish for disagreeing.
2. Opinions must be supported with logic and proof that they are correct. Feelings don't count.
3. Wear your opponents down with logic until they lose control of themselves, which then proves your point.
4. Keep mirroring the faults of the other person so that no one will notice yours.
5. Hide your shame by acting superior. A good co-dependent will express your feelings for you, and you will walk away looking great.

Another expression of perfectionism in communication is in those who just don't talk because they have convinced themselves that they can't do it right. They expect to be overpowered and lose every argument. (They too believe winning is the goal.) They think, prepare, plan and edit every response, while their partner has bowled them over. They then feel ashamed and stupid for not expressing themselves as well as they should.

When we use our communication to protect and defend ourselves, more than to share who we are with each other, it is no wonder our relationships and our self-esteem suffer. We also forget that half of communicating is listening, so we don't make the time for this to happen. The mental clatter and frenetic activity of the perfectionist do not allow for either.

This chapter has given most of the bad news about perfectionism and co-dependency, yet despite their awareness of its effects, many will cling to the belief that it is better than letting go and feeling the fear. It is important to view it from a larger, family perspective in order to understand that we did not get this way alone, and we don't have to work through it alone.

4

How Did I Get To Be So Good?

It would be gross oversimplification to assume that every-thing about us is determined by our family environment as children. As in the case of obsessive-compulsive disease, many of our assets and defects — more than we will ever know — are actually physiological. It is now believed that personality has a great deal to do with genetics. This would be true whether we grew up in a healthy family or a dysfunctional one. When one of our natural characteristics becomes com-pulsive, it is related to emotional pain.

Society also has a strong influence. We live in an addictive society which continually sends us messages about our need to be perfect, to get the quick fix, to look good, to feel good. We are encouraged by advertising and social institutions to not feel what we feel, to evaluate the quality of our lives by material wealth, to expend enormous amounts of energy in attaining the perfect body or the perfect house, while our emotional and spiritual self dies from lack of care.

Our early school experiences may set us up for perfectionism with the slogans, "Do Your Best" and "Anything Worth Doing Is Worth Doing Well." Often school systems are designed for one type of student, one pattern of learning. Those who don't adjust are stigmatized as learning disabled. The world we live in is sadly ignorant about such important things as feelings, intimacy, parenting, self-worth and so on.

A pervasive denial exists concerning the importance of our relationships with each other and our impact on our children. I watched with wonder a popular talk show focusing on the issue of children who had been adopted after having been abused by their birth parents. The adoptive parents were very kind, caring people who adopted these children in the belief that today is all that matters in the life of the child. They were shocked to discover that these children were showing the effects of their abuse emotionally and behaviorally years later, despite the dedicated efforts of the adoptive parents.

What amazed me was the prevailing myth that the past has nothing to do with the present, that what a child does not actually remember will not have lasting effects. I have encountered the same denial in my work with co-dependents and ACoAs. Adults who are struggling with such issues as perfectionism blame themselves and can't imagine why they cannot just stop their dysfunctional behavior.

There is no doubt that we are strongly influenced by our family background. We cannot look only at one generation to examine the effects, however, since each of our parents also brings an emotional legacy into our family. Children in pain become adults in pain; but we learn to hide it from others and ourselves.

To illustrate, I would like to share a story with you of three generations who did the best that they could with what they had.

A Tale Of Three Families

Once upon a time two young couples, the Joneses and the

O'Learys, lived in a small New England town. Although they were raised in the same community, they appeared to be from very different worlds. They lived under sharply contrasting moral, social and economic standards. They had nothing in common — so they believed.

The Joneses

The Joneses were a couple everyone admired. Jeff Jones was the pastor of the largest church in the community. He was a handsome, well dressed, upstanding man who worked long hours without complaint, serving both his congregation and the town through active involvement on boards and citizen's groups.

On a personal level Jeff was very controlled and controlling. He knew the right way to do most anything — from driving a car to life in general. He never lost his temper and was perceived as a man who could support others through crisis but would never have one himself. When he was angry or upset, Jeff was ashamed and felt weak and out of control. He used his work to avoid this discomfort.

Jeff had very strong opinions about how others should live and behave. In private, particularly at home, he did not hesitate to criticize. After a few glasses of wine he would loosen up and talk more freely, but always about the deficiencies of others, including his wife, Joann. Jeff really had two lives, the public and the private.

Joann Jones was an attractive woman with a pleasant smile — outside of the home. She was very conscious of the image she was projecting to others and didn't want to offend anyone or make a social error. Joann had a part-time job that did not interfere with her household and social/church responsibilities.

In the home Joann was very busy with a list of duties. She did not choose to do these things, they were expected of her by others. She secretly resented the back seat she took to her husband but never let on that this bothered her. After all, this was the woman's role: to support and make life easier for her husband. She enjoyed the attention they received from the congregation and the status of being the pastor's wife. But secretly she said to herself, "If they only knew him, they wouldn't admire him." If her "nerves" got bad, Joann had a prescription from the doctor to calm her.

The Joneses were seen as the perfect couple, although perhaps a little stiff, and they never argued. Among friends they might tease a little and poke sarcastically at one another's faults, but they never had a fight.

The unspoken standards that guided the Joneses were not terribly spiritual, despite their church involvement. They were:

- You are what you do.
- Think.
- If you look good, you are good.
- Maintain control (don't feel).
- Don't tell.
- Do the right thing.

The Joneses eventually had a son, their only child, named Jeffrey Jr. Little Jeffrey was a jovial, curious child, into everything. He loved to draw, especially on the walls; but he received quick disapproval for that and any other "inappropriate" behavior. Jeffrey had to learn to control his urges, or else he would be scolded and rejected by his mother. Sometimes, when Mom was particularly upset with Dad, she would be very critical of Jeffrey Jr.

He saw very little of Dad, but as he was growing up people often told Jeffrey what a good man his father was and how lucky he was to be in this family. Mom, on the other hand, did not seem to be too fond of Dad, although she never really said that.

Jeffrey was a good student and athlete. He had a few friends, carefully screened by Mom for their acceptability. People thought of him as a good person, intelligent and active. Jeffrey had a few disappointments in his life. For instance, he was not allowed to play football, although he was very good at it, and he was pressured into an accelerated academic program even though he didn't feel as smart as the other kids in it. When he told his parents how he felt, they told him not to feel that way and that they knew best. After a while he stopped having those feelings and just complied with their expectations.

Sometimes Jeffrey would try especially hard at something with the hope that his father would notice and give him some attention. Mostly, however, Dad found fault and continued to push. But overall Jeffrey had anything he needed and felt very prepared for life. If anyone asked, he said — and believed, "Everything is great!"

The O'Learys

The O'Learys had a very different sort of home. They lived in a lower-middle-class neighborhood. Mike was a laborer who had difficulty finding and keeping work because he was an alcoholic. When he was sober, Mike was quiet and a bit depressed. When he drank, he rarely came home. When he was at home, he was angry and sometimes violent.

Mike O'Leary was an avid bowler. All of his friends bowled and they spent many nights each week at the bowling alley. He almost never came home when he was expected. He spent money on beer, bowling and betting on games. The family was suffering because of this. Mike and his wife, Maureen, had terrible fights about Mike's bowling and his friends. The fights were loud and sometimes the neighbors would call the police.

Mike appeared to be totally self-centered and insensitive to those around him. He frequently blamed his wife for his absences and his drinking. He threatened to leave, saying she could not survive without him, but he never did.

Maureen had hoped to be taken care of by the wonderful man she first knew. When they met, he was a bit wild but a lot of fun. Time had taken its toll, however, and it seemed that Mike would never change. Both Mike and Maureen came from alcoholic families. They didn't expect much from life. To Maureen happiness would have been having a husband who didn't hit her and brought a paycheck home.

Maureen was a nurse's aid in a nursing home, taking care of sick and elderly patients on the night shift. She was preoc-cupied while she was at work with the thought that something terrible would happen at home. For a while she called home frequently but would only end up fighting with Mike on the phone. Over time she began to lose hope and harden in her anger. She just didn't care anymore. Having a husband — even one like Mike — was better than being alone.

When she was younger, Maureen left Mike a few times. But he would promise to change and she always came back for the children. At home and around her own family Maureen complained endlessly about Mike. She truly believed that if only he would change, she would be fine. Maureen used food for comfort and became obese over the years. She did not care about her appearance or about the house. She slept as much as she could because she didn't have to feel when she was asleep.

Mike and Maureen had three children, Peggy, Todd and Linda. When Peggy was born, Mike and Maureen were unprepared, since they had only been dating a few months when Maureen got pregnant. Maureen had hopes that the baby would help to settle Mike down, keeping him home more often. Peggy was a pleasant child, smiling, cooperative and quiet. She did not demand much and was seen as independent and capable.

As Mike's drinking increased, the arguments often centered on his feeling pressured because Maureen insisted on having children and was always too tired to have sex or keep him company. In Peggy's mind that meant he went out and drank because of her. At a very early age Peggy began to take care of her mother.

Often after an argument, even when Peggy was only three or four, Maureen would be in the kitchen crying and depressed. Peggy would brush her mother's hair and tell her it would be OK, "Daddy will be home soon." Maureen would be grateful for the support and say, "I don't know what I'd do without you." For that brief moment Peggy felt important and not alone. She learned that if you take care of others and are very good, sometimes they will give you something back.

As she grew up Peggy became aware that other children did not have homes like hers. She and her brother and sister lay in bed terrified of the sounds downstairs, not daring to say a word, even to each other. She began to develop a fantasy of the day when she would leave home and create the kind of family she saw on television and in her friends' houses.

Peggy was an excellent student. She often was chosen for special tasks in the classroom, tutored other children and was active in most anything she could find. When she came home, Peggy cleaned the house, cooked and took care of her brother and sister. She discovered that the busier she was, the less depressed she felt. As long as she didn't make any mistakes she was fine. In fact she received much praise — outside of her home. She never believed it though, since she knew who she really was and they didn't. If she failed at something, said the wrong thing or disappointed someone, she was devastated and ashamed. She would avoid people, work harder and focus on other people's problems.

Peggy survived on the belief that someday she would do it differently, the "right way." Peggy dreamed about being a doctor but decided to become a nurse and to have a perfect family of her own.

Todd and Linda survived each in their own way. Todd could not compete with his older sister and got more attention from being the family problem child. Todd struggled with anything he did. He fought with other children in nursery school and continued this pattern throughout his school years. The more stressful things were at home, the more he would act out. Ironically Todd felt rejected but continued to push people away and blame them for not wanting him.

Todd found marijuana when he was 14 and medicated himself, blaming his drunk father, from that point on. Peggy did everything she could to stop him, but he strongly resented her meddling and did not want another parent. Todd's parents found him to be a convenient scapegoat and focused on him as the primary problem in the home.

Linda became invisible. She found safety in her isolation and felt better when she didn't know what was going on. Linda loved her stuffed aminals and her pet bird. She spent most of her time in her room or eating while she watched television. She did not bother anyone and remained average and unnoticed throughout her childhood. Peggy felt responsible for her little sister but did not know how to help her.

Peggy And Jeffrey

Two very attractive, intelligent people meet on a blind date. Peggy knew exactly what she was looking for in a future mate — the opposite of Dad, responsible, secure, light drinker, hard working and emotionally stable. Jeffrey was just starting law school and had a bright future ahead of him. Although he was a good conversationalist, Peggy had a hard time figuring him out. She found this to be a challenge, however, and decided that in time he would relax and share himself with her. She especially liked his family — they looked so normal and healthy. He was exactly what she wanted.

Jeffrey had never thought for one moment about what he wanted in a wife (except that she should fit in with his life-style), but he was immediately attracted to Peggy. He felt a little sorry for her with her messed-up family, but he also liked the challenge of it. Jeffrey's parents were not particularly pleased with his choice and for once that felt good too. Peggy looked great and knew how to fit in, and when he was with her he felt a bit superior. When she started to talk about marriage and children, he went along even though he'd never thought about this very much. Jeffrey was busy planning his career.

Once they were married they just knew things would work out. Peggy was determined enough for both of them. She got a job as a nurse in the emergency room, working part time so that she also could work on decorating their home and being supportive to Jeffrey. She created the perfect home and they looked like the perfect couple.

They made a silent pact about three very important things:

1. The past is the past — I won't ask you if you don't ask me.
2. I'll do what's expected of me but don't ask me to be vulnerable.
3. Peggy will do all the feeling, Jeffrey will do all the thinking.

They ran into a few difficulties early on in their relationship, but nothing they couldn't overlook. Peggy tended to overreact to small things — at least that's what Jeffrey said.

Actually she would hold her feelings in as long as she could and then blow up.

Often their discussions (not arguments, since good couples don't argue) about his lack of communication and affection would result in Peggy getting hysterical while Jeffrey became increasingly rational. Since Jeffrey was not in touch with his feelings, he didn't know what she was talking about. To her frequent question of, "Well, do you love me?" He would respond, "Of course I do. I married you, didn't I?"

Jeffrey never felt the actual feeling of love, but had some idea about what he was supposed to do. Every once in a while he would kiss her for no reason or bring her flowers. Peggy would then ask, "What do you want now?"

They both knew this wasn't exactly what they expected from marriage, but it was OK. What they needed was a distraction from each other.

Children would be the perfect distraction, thought Peggy, and she felt very competent in this area. Jeffrey was in favor of having children but left the parenting to Peggy. This was just as well, since Peggy was hardly a team player and preferred to do it alone. She had spent years watching her mother mess up and was determined to be the opposite kind of mom. Where her mother had been weak and unreliable, Peggy would be strong and always available. Where her mother was not affectionate and didn't talk to her children, Peggy would tell them she loved them every day and communicate with them. Peggy wanted what she thought others had and attempted to give it all to her children.

Her daughter, Kelly, and her son, Jason, were three years apart so that she could spend the proper amount of time with each in their infancy. She avoided giving her children any unnatural foods and relied on breastfeeding and homemade baby foods. She used only cloth diapers because she had always been very concerned about the environment. Peggy believed it was very important to read to her children every day and felt guilty when she wasn't able to do this.

Kelly and Jason took piano lessons but Jason switched to violin — the Suzuki method, where Peggy participated in his lessons. They also played soccer and softball and each was on several teams. They were a very busy family, out almost every night with some activity. Peggy was in the PTA and eventually became president. She was an active environmentalist in the community, lobbying for legislation to mandate recycling.

The family also was involved in the church, singing in the choir, serving on committees as needed and helping with fund-raising events.

Peggy and Jeffrey had not exactly left their families and had regular contact with both sides. Peggy's mother called her daily for continued moral support and to remind her that she had abandoned them. Her brother, Todd, was in more serious trouble these days and needed some financial help; and Linda had recently attempted suicide. Peggy continued to feel responsible and guilty for leaving but kept as much as possible from her children. Kelly and Jason did not know their grandfather was an alcoholic and they would never find out from Peggy.

Jeffrey's family came over every Sunday for dinner. They expressed their hostility to Peggy indirectly through sarcasm and asides about her housekeeping, asking her about her father and other sensitive subjects. When Peggy would ask Jeffrey to intervene for her, he acted as if he didn't notice anything. The Joneses were actually wonderful with Kelly and Jason, which made Peggy feel even more inadequate.

Jeffrey's career really began to take off. Peggy blamed this for the deterioration of their marriage, but held to the hope that relief was over the next hill. When Jeffrey had an affair, Peggy buried herself in the intensity of her work and her volunteer activities. She was preoccupied with her parents but felt helpless to do anything other than rescue and lecture as she needed to. Any time spent away from the children for any reason caused her to feel guilty. She wasn't doing enough and needed to try harder.

Jason and Kelly were Looking Good children. Peggy liked them to be well dressed and well groomed. Underneath the facade, however, Jason had a learning disability, which kept Peggy busy visiting the school and working with him on his reading. She took it personally when Jason struggled and he began to hide his problems from her because of her over-reaction.

Kelly was overweight, which was very disturbing to Peggy. She seemed like a happy child but Peggy continued to focus on her flaws, as if it were a reflection on her parenting. Kelly became very manipulative. Although she was never outwardly angry she knew exactly how to get her mother upset. Eating was one effective way.

Jason and Kelly believed, and had been told, that they were very lucky children. They were told they were loved every day and they had everything they could want. When they were sick they got a great deal of attention; but their mother was very busy most of the time and did not share much with them. Dad was absent, working hard to take care of them.

Peggy became increasingly stressed with her chaotic life. One day she was confronted with almost everything at once. She went to work at the hospital emergency room feeling agitated after discovering that her son was going to be held back a grade level in school. At work she received a phone call from her mother, who was crying after being threatened by her father. She could not let any of this interfere with her work, so she just put it in the back of her mind and told no one how upset she was. She would deal with it all later.

During the afternoon an elderly man came in to the emergency room with a gash on his head from having fallen down the stairs, drunk. Peggy lost it. She let him wait as long as possible, screamed at him, "Don't you know what you're doing to your family?" and treated him abruptly and roughly.

Her co-workers were shocked. Peggy had never lost control before. She was devastated and ashamed.

Fortunately, in tears, Peggy confided in a friend at work. This person recommended a book to read and suggested an ACoA meeting. Peggy was desperate enough to try anything. Through her new search, which she attacked with the same zeal with which she conducted her environmental campaign, Peggy began to see the unmanageability in her life and her family. She began treatment for co-dependency. In time Peggy realized that she had become her mother, but was grateful that today she had many more choices than her mother had.

Peggy came to a realization that she (and her mother) had done the very best she knew how, giving everything she had but she could not overcome the painful legacy of her family. It was no one's fault.

Blocks To Healthy Relationships

These families seem familiar? Although we all have different, somewhat unique experiences, we have much in common as human beings. Whether we resemble the Joneses or the O'Learys, we were all children once with the same emotional needs. For many those needs are not met. Each of the individuals in the above story has a child inside whose needs were unnoticed. They were each raised by another starving needy child who learned to adapt to his or her surroundings, living on what little love and nurturing was available.

Becoming a perfect child is one way to adapt to a painful family experience. Certainly Jeff and Joann learned that doing it right gave them some comfort if not self-worth. Peggy and Jeffrey, in their attempts at looking good, were hoping eventually to feel good in the process. They had become accustomed to seeking from others what they were lacking in themselves.

Perfectionism is not present at birth. It develops as a response to stress, which is then positively reinforced by others. Several issues prevent adequate emotional maturation for children and adults from painful families. Although unknown to the individual, these handicaps become blocks to healthy relationships and are then passed on to the next generation.

Lack Of Trust

At birth we are as perfect as we are supposed to be. There is nothing about us that is unlovable or in need of change, until we encounter parents with a multitude of unresolved problems of their own. Peggy was a beautiful, perfect child who was forced to adapt to the family she was born into.

As an infant Peggy knew instinctively that she would not survive unless she had some kind of connection with her mother or father. She learned through trial and error what it would take to become connected and how to maintain it.

At this time in her fragile life she was learning about trust. Will they feed me when I'm hungry, change me when I'm wet, hold me gently when I cry, smile back at me when I smile? Is this world a safe, predictable, consistent place? The answer for Peggy and many others is no. When we have parents whose basic needs for things such as safety, intimacy and consistency are not met, they cannot give what they do not have. At best we are cared for by stressful hands, feeling and hearing tension. We may even discover that when we behave in a particular way, the tension goes away.

Infants are capable of learning from their experiences. With continued reinforcement and repetition we find a behavior that works. If we cannot trust our environment the way it is, maybe we can learn to control it. The need to control is always a response to fear. The ultimate fear for both the child and adult is fear of abandonment, which from the infant's perspective means death. In my work with ACoAs and other co-dependents I frequently meet adults who carry with them irrational fears of being alone. These fears are truly rooted in very early childhood experiences.

The perfect child (often the firstborn) has discovered that the better you are, the more you get. Parents of a perfect child, even if they are hurting, will gain some relief early in a child's life from their achievements. They are loved for doing, not for being. The message they get from a positive parental response to their behavior is, "You make me feel like a good parent when you walk at 10 months! Do more!"

When a child whose emotional needs are not consistently met receives such a wonderful response for doing something well, he will do it often. The excitement of the first steps or smile or reading cannot sustain a family in pain, and so the validation becomes less frequent. They learn to survive on crumbs and not to expect much from others.

In addition to inconsistencies in behavior, a child also may experience confusion as a result of parents saying one thing and doing another. Peggy, for example, grew up with the dishonesty characteristic of an alcoholic family. Jeffrey also learned to not trust words, since he often felt internally the anger that was hidden behind the tight smiles of his parents.

The inability to trust leads children to begin their lives in a defensive posture. "I know I'm going to be hurt, so I'd better take care of myself." Becoming a perfectionist is one very effective way to do this.

Lack Of Intimacy

It is clear from our tale of three families that although these people lived in close proximity to one another, they were unable to be truly intimate. There are a number of reasons for this difficulty:

1. They have never seen or felt intimacy and don't know how to achieve it.
2. Each person is to some degree shame-based — that is, they feel "less than" others and fear being abandoned if they are found out.
3. They have "chosen" (the term is used loosely here, since co-dependents don't really make choices) mates who could not be intimate, even if they themselves were able.
4. They have been around non-intimate people — meaning friends, family and so on — for so long that they believe what they are experiencing is normal.
5. People who do not know their own feelings and cannot express them will never be intimate.

Intimacy is an honest emotional connection between two human beings. The intimacy between parent and child will of course be very different from that between adult friends, or lovers. At least five ingredients are necessary for intimacy to occur.

1. There must be an "I" to share. We have to know clearly who we are before we can share ourselves with someone else.
2. We must be able to face the possibility that with our honesty may come rejection. Intimate relationships are

not without conflict. The connection comes from sharing without defensiveness, the good and the bad.

3. Intimacy is not about sharing opinions or activities, although that will be part of it. It is about sharing feelings — about life, about myself, about you. Feelings are such things as sadness, fear, anger, guilt, shame and joy.

4. Clear boundaries give us a sense of safety. When I know where I begin and you end, I do not hold you responsible for my feelings. I do not ask you to be my sole support. I do not need to know everything about you. I don't place excessive demands, nor will I tolerate abuse.

5. Interdependence suggests a willingness to both give to and receive from the other.

Many of us fear intimacy because of the risks involved in getting that close. Co-dependents often tell stories of running from what seemed to be a healthy person because they felt threatened. Sex is often used to avoid intimacy: "You can have my body, as long as I don't have to tell you who I am."

Perfectionism causes us to look competent, self-sufficient and complete. By using it as a defense the characters in our story — Jeff, Joann, Jeffrey and Peggy — prevented others from reaching out to them. Ironically, in seeking approval so diligently, they actually prevented anyone from filling their need for love and connection.

Lack Of Identity

Each of us is born with a clear sense of who we are and where we're supposed to be going. It is demonstrated to us and to others, especially our parents, in our personalities, interests, curiosities, physical abilities and so on. When I was an infant, for example, I cried very loudly. My movements often were attention-seeking, energetic and a little hyper. As I have grown to love and accept who I am, I have realized that I was preparing to be a public speaker. My work is much more than work; it is an opportunity to use my God-given gifts to my own pleasure and to make a contribution to others.

The trick as parents is to allow our children to just be, providing structure and safety while they evolve into their full potential. It would be rare to find someone who had a perfect environment where this occurred without anything hampering self-actualization.

Jeffrey Junior, the son of two rigid, repressed perfectionists, did not have a chance to find out who he was. In order to be connected to and accepted by his parents, he had to be what they expected. Very early in his life he began to give up parts of himself. As an adult, even though he was very successful, he never felt any satisfaction with his work or his relationships. He had developed a pseudo-self — in a sense he was having an "out-of-body" experience. He was unable to look inside at any moment and ask himself the question, "Is this what I want to be doing?"

Children who live in a painful family are not asked who they are. Parents believe they are responsible for designing their children and force certain acceptable standards and even preferences on children. Jeffrey was not asked, "Who are you? What do you like to eat? Would you rather play football or piano?" He complied with the rules and lost himself in the process.

Sadly it seems that children such as Jeffrey and Peggy, and their children, do what they have to do to survive with the least amount of pain. By the time they reach the crisis that drives them to examine themselves (this may be called a midlife crisis, severe depression or the end of a relationship) they have no sense of who they are and will need treatment to begin the search for the lost child.

Perfectionism can be a substitute, although an ineffective one, for identity. We may begin to define ourselves by the roles we play and judge ourselves based on how perfectly we play them. The greater the need to be perfect, the weaker the identity of the person within.

Shame

Shame is perhaps the single greatest factor contributing to perfectionism. When a child feels flawed — remember that in families such as Peggy's, she believes she caused the problem

— she needs to compensate for the sense of worthlessness. She believed that she was not loved because she wasn't good enough. In painful families children have three basic choices in response to the stress:

1. *Compliance* with what they believe is expected of them. This is often the choice of the firstborn. He or she will find out what the rules are (even if they keep changing) and try to follow them. The complier who gets occasional positive results probably will develop this as a lifetime pattern, but not necessarily.

2. *Rebellion* against anything that appears to be rigid or authoritarian. There are many forms of rebellion — some quiet and thoughtful, some outward and defiant. Often if the firstborn has opted for compliance, a second child, like Todd, may find rebellion to be more effective. We will do whatever it takes to be attended to. If negative behavior gets the focus of the family, we may use it.

   The complier and the rebel may switch roles at any time.

3. *Becoming invisible* is another way to survive. The invisible child, like Linda in our story, will find safety within herself. She will develop an ability to "go inside" to a safe place and actually tune out the stress. This child also may be skilled at not being noticed, wearing drab colors, speaking quietly, avoiding eye contact, being average in every way. Most of us will recall a period in our lives when we withdrew; some have done it for a lifetime.

Often we will assume that the Looking Good child, the complier, has high self-worth. All three of these roles represent children, and later adults, who are shame-based. They have found ways to cover their inadequacies and to protect themselves with an armor of compulsive behavior.

Perfectionists struggle internally with the knowledge that if they show a flaw in a particular area which they have focused on, to others or to themselves, they will be seen as worthless and rejected. Thoughts like, "What will others think of me?" "How could I have done that?" "I am bad," are continually

buzzing in the mind of the perfectionist. This feeling is sometimes called guilt but in reality it is shame. Guilt is a response
to having made a mistake. Shame is a feeling, deep within, of
actually *being* a mistake. Guilt is short lived; shame stays with
us for a long time, and often it is medicated with chemicals or
compulsive behavior.

The issues of trust, intimacy, identity and shame are major
areas of retarded development for the co-dependent. The good
news is that it is never too late to begin the process of change.
We are capable of growing in each of these areas — fortunately at a much faster rate than in childhood.

5

Overcoming Perfectionism: Learning To Live In The Middle

Letting Go Of The Myth — The Pitfalls And Benefits

The decision to become more human — less perfect — is not an easy one to make, despite the fact that we know we have been trying to accomplish the impossible.

Before you make a commitment to this change, I'd like to suggest a brief exercise. Stop for a moment and make two lists: a list of the advantages of living as a perfectionist, and a list of the pitfalls. Then rate each item on a scale of 1 to 5 according to its overall importance or value in your life (1 indicates little importance, 5 is very important to you). Most perfectionists will find this part very difficult. My personal list may be helpful as a guide:

Benefits Of Remaining A Perfectionist	Rating
1. I get to feel superior at times.	1
2. I accomplish a great deal in little time.	4
3. People look up to me for support and help.	3
4. I have succeeded professionally using this method.	4
5. My life is often orderly, structured and sensible.	4
6. I have a fleeting sense of control over life.	2
7. I get strokes for looking superhuman.	2
	20

Pitfalls Of Being A Perfectionist	Rating
1. I can be very isolated when I am being perfect.	5
2. I don't have enough quiet time because I'm always doing.	4
3. I am in the role of leader more than I like.	3
4. My parenting becomes rigid and critical when I try to be perfect.	5
5. I suffer from physical effects of the stress I impose on myself.	5
6. If I look like I superwoman, that's what others expect of me.	5
7. I take on responsibility that isn't mine, believing others can't do it as well.	4
8. It isn't fun.	5
	36

You may find that the benefits of staying perfectionistic outnumber the pitfalls, but you probably will discover that the benefits have less value or significance in your life. Our reasons for hanging on to this compulsion don't make much sense when we compare them to qualities like intimacy, peace of mind, joy, good parenting and so on.

You make the decision to give up your perfectionism one day, even one moment at a time. It is something you may not be able to adhere to consistently but view as an overall goal. Since recovery is not an intellectual process, this decision is an important but very small first step. You will make it many times over through the days and years ahead.

Do I Really Need To Change?

Whenever I speak before an audience on the subject of co-dependency, people inevitably have questions about their spouses, children and friends who have the characteristics I am discussing. They want very much for the other person to change, often out of love but also out of frustration. Living with a perfectionist or any compulsive person is not easy. Others generally see our problem long before we do.

Unfortunately the frustration of others is rarely strong enough motivation for us to begin the long, uncomfortable process of change. You will probably not be able to sustain the effort for someone else.

I do not believe that being co-dependent or perfectionistic automatically means that one needs treatment. Unless our lives become unmanageable as described in chapter 3, and we want very much to have a different life, we will not benefit from treatment. If we are in denial of severe consequences and others lovingly point them out to us, perhaps in a formal intervention, we may be able to feel a personal need and begin the process.

When we try to diagnose others (with the exception of those in severe physical or emotional crises and in denial), it is usually our *own* compulsive behavior that we are struggling with.

If you are on the fence about whether or not this issue is an important one for you, ask three people who care about you whether or not they think your perfectionism is a problem. If they agree that it is, pay attention to this old AA saying: "If it walks like a duck and talks like a duck, it's a duck." Try surrendering and take it one step at a time.

Changing From The Inside Out

Many perfectionists have spent their lives trying to look OK. This presents a problem in early treatment and recovery. Others will not always acknowledge our pain, and may even tell us we're fine because we appear to be. Recovery requires changing our insides so that they match up with our outsides. This means looking sad when you are sad, getting tired when you have worked hard, having needs, being vulnerable. It cannot be accomplished simply by reading books or studying the behavior of others (that was one of my personal favorites).

Many perfectionists experience extreme difficulty when they try to get in touch with how they feel. We may even reach a point where we don't know when we're tired, unless someone points it out to us; and we certainly cannot acknowledge, even to ourselves, that we need anything.

We have learned to look like people with high self-worth, while internally we feel like we're not as good as others. Our self-esteem has become conditional. We feel OK about ourselves when we do everything up to standard, have the list completed, achieve the perfect weight and so on. Whenever we judge ourselves based on outside standards, or even by comparing our insides to other people's outsides, we will be uncomfortable. Perfectionists always assume that those who look good feel good.

The true healing and lasting change will not come from improving what we look like or sound like to others. Our problem is with our internal feelings and voices. In fact one sign of recovery is the willingness to look foolish or make a mistake and still feel good about who we are.

There are many ways to recover, and as many places to do it, but the following three stages of treatment and recovery are most common: (1) identification, (2) expression of pain and (3) understanding, letting go and forgiving.

Stage I: Identification

The act of reading this book is an attempt to identify or name the difficulties you may be experiencing in your life.

Giving the problem a name is useful at this stage and brings some relief from the guilt and shame of struggling alone. You did not get this way all by yourself. You are part of a family and a world that helped you along. You have chosen a particular compulsive behavior that served you well but it no longer makes sense.

Many others have the same problem, and we even can laugh at the absurdity of trying to be perfect. You are not alone. This is good news!

You will learn many important things during the identification stage. Much of this you can get on your own from reading, talking and listening to others, perhaps at self-help meetings or in another support group. Co-dependents get a great deal of support and take a giant leap forward when they begin to share with each other.

Because you are open to it, you will find some things you are glad to discover and others you'd rather not know. This is all part of the process. Some examples:

- You may realize that your children have been hurt by what you thought was excellent parenting.
- You may find that the family you were raised in was abusive. You now know what abuse is.
- You remember painful events in your marriage and see that they are much like what you saw between your parents as a child.
- You discover that you are a very critical person and feel ashamed of it.
- You find that you have new choices since you've learned that you can change anything about yourself if you're willing to work at it.
- You talk to old friends and find that while some of them don't want you to be imperfect, others have wanted to reach out to you but didn't know how.

You learn simple but new concepts like: Feelings aren't bad or good. It helps to talk. You are important.

Memories will start to surface but often they bring a great deal of confusion. Everything you once thought you understood has been reframed to look like something else. Perfectionism felt like an asset, now it's a defect. You don't know if you can trust your own perceptions anymore. You may trust that the new things you are hearing from your support system feel right inside, and you may temporarily become dependent on others for a "reality check."

Pain will begin to surface with the realization of abuse experienced in the past. The immediate temptation is to avoid the pain by denying, minimizing, forgetting or even focusing more on what we have done to others, especially our children. It is necessary to begin with what was done to us. This is a short visit into a painful past, not something we will dwell on, blaming and wallowing for months or years. The goal is to feel it now and move through it.

Most co-dependents have little or no awareness of what abuse is. Those who come from severe abuse tend to believe that anything other than physical abuse is normal and acceptable. Those who come from Looking Good families have received good physical care but may have been emotionally abused. I define abuse as any behavior that intentionally or unintentionally decreases the self-esteem of another. Some of the subtle abuses faced in the Identification stage are: emotional neglect, shame as discipline, praise without affirmation, boundary abuses and repression of feelings.

Emotional Neglect

It is abusive to have parents who expected you, as a child, to take care of yourself or to clearly express your needs before you were able. Parents have the responsibility to seek out and meet the needs of a child. Often parents who were abused as children are starving, needy children themselves. They do not have much to give because their own needs have been unmet.

Children may be cared for physically but overlooked when they are in pain. They may be punished for crying or acting out, which are the only means of communication for a hurting child. This neglect in childhood leads to a lifetime of abandonment. Many co-dependents continue to live with emotional neglect in their adult relationships and have very low expectations of others who are significant to them.

Shame As Discipline

Many forms of discipline widely believed to be good for the child are extremely damaging. Physical and sexual abuse tell the child that he or she is worthless, an object with no feelings. Both are very shaming and take away our boundaries. But verbal abuse can also be shaming. In an effort to gain the respect of their children many hurting parents use words as weapons, believing that a child will forget and recover quickly from such abuse.

As children, perfectionists often heard such statements as:

- You'll never be good enough.
- Why can't you be like your brother?
- Is that the best you can do?
- Why didn't you get an A?
- Sit up straight, dress right, talk right, be what I want you to be.
- What will people think?

Many heard themselves called worthless, whore, slut, loser, good for nothing and worse.

Shaming also can take a more subtle form. Parents or caregivers, including teachers, may use nonverbal means to control behavior. An example is a look of disgust, withdrawal or silence because the child has made a mistake. Another example is guilting a child by saying, "How could you do this to me?" and acting as if the child's error is destroying your life, making you sick and so on. Children internalize the feeling that they are only lovable if they are perfect, whatever that is. The perfect child keeps trying to earn love.

Praise Without Affirmation

Looking Good families often try to make children into successful achievers. Unfortunately the motivation of the parent may be to make himself or herself feel good as a parent, rather than to give the children opportunities to feel good about themselves. Self-worth does not come from the outside. Praise is attached to doing things that please parents. It is necessary for us to learn to feel good when we do nothing as well as when we achieve.

In an effort to be a good parent Mom or Dad may give praise and rewards for doing, accomplishing, succeeding and so on, but neglect to affirm and validate the worth of the child. The only way to get more praise is to do more. Many children learn to wait a very long time from one moment of praise to the next, perhaps years. Affirmation needs to be there on a daily basis. We need to hear, "I see you, I like you, I'm glad you are my child, I love you no matter what you do."

The combination of praise and affirmation will give us self-worth. Praise alone deprives us of good feelings about ourselves. It is abusive to be loved only when you are meeting the needs of a parent.

Boundary Abuses

Healthy boundaries help us to feel safe. They make it possible for us to be intimate without losing ourselves in the process. When we are raised by parents who do not know how to teach boundaries, abuse and victimization result. Examples of subtle boundary abuse may include:

- *Role reversals.* Janet's mother said with pride, "Janet and I are very close, I can tell her anything. We are like sisters." Children need parents to be parents. Many parents tell their children about their adult problems and seek support from the child.
- *Smothering.* Giving affection or other physical contact without the child's approval.
- *Telling children* what they like, how they feel, what their needs are without input from the child.
- *Lack of privacy* or personal space.
- *Enmeshment* or forced togetherness with parents, family or siblings.

- *Adult-centered families* where the parents' needs and preferences are the only ones considered. Children are ignored or seen as little adults.

Repression Of Feelings

In families with severe abuse it is a brilliant survival tool to keep one's feelings to oneself. In mildly dysfunctional families there is no need to repress feelings to prevent violence. Even so, in such families the rules of several generations of painful families may continue to apply.

When appropriate expression of feelings is not modeled or even permitted, children are left with handicaps in many areas of their lives. People in Looking Good families appear to be in control and may even look happy. But painful feelings lie just beneath the glossy surface with no healthy outlet.

Being unable to identify or express feelings prevents an individual from ever connecting in an intimate way with other human beings. It is abusive to be deprived of this essential skill for interpersonal relationships. Compulsive behavior and stress-related illness are also consequences of repression of feelings. Our parents did the best they could with what they had. Unfortunately they lacked the skills and tools to teach us how to address feelings. Their helplessness does not remove the long-term negative effects.

The identification stage tends to be a negative one, and we are tempted to jump ahead and forgive without allowing ourselves to feel what we feel about it.

Although you see more clearly what is wrong and have some sense of what needs to change, you are still unable to do it. The next step will take a great leap of faith: In order to move from an intellectual awareness of your problems to truly changing and recovering, means feeling the pain of the past.

Stage II: Expression Of Pain

The second stage in the treatment and recovery process is that of expression of painful feelings. Most of us have spent a lifetime trying to avoid these feelings and the consequences of burying them are often what bring us into treatment. This stage cannot be bypassed.

Joseph's experience is a typical example. After three years of sobriety and some recent education about co-dependency, Joseph decided he would like to be an alcoholism counselor. He was very intelligent and empathetic, and had excellent instincts when he helped others in recovery. Joseph felt great when he received positive results and feedback as he guided and supported others in his 12-Step group.

Although Joseph was an abused child, he had never explored the impact of this trauma on his adult life. He believed it was irrelevant as long as he was sober. At the recommendation of his friends in AA, Joseph dove into his new career, putting the past behind him. Within two years of his employment as a counselor in a treatment center, however, Joseph was overwhelmed, overworked and "burning out." His role as a counselor, focusing on the problems of others, developed into a new addiction. He had become a workaholic and his personal life was totally out of control again. Joseph could not run fast enough to avoid the pain of his past. He did not break this compulsive pattern until he reluctantly faced the abuses and pain of his childhood and past adult life.

The most frequently repressed and problematic feelings in recovery are anger, grief, fear and shame. Each of us has our own emotional response to life. But when we have lived in a dysfunctional family without healthy emotional release, it is common to struggle with each of these to some extent. The intensity and order of appearance may differ but most of us will encounter each at some point in the recovery process.

Anger: Old And New

When Joseph hit bottom with his co-dependency, he was raging most of the time. His crisis on the job was primarily due to his angry outbursts and impatience with other staff and patients. At first he believed it was the fault of his employer, but gradually he became aware that he was angry everywhere, regardless of the source. As an abused child Joseph was not allowed to express his anger. He had developed a lifetime pattern of "stuffing it" and smiling it away. He was a nice guy with a very short fuse. He needed professional help.

Joseph's treatment process began with a somewhat negative emphasis. In a weekly therapy group he was given the opportunity to focus on the past and even on blaming to some extent. Joseph was very uncomfortable with this stage and wanted to move into forgiving his parents as quickly as possible. His 12-Step program had encouraged him to live in the present without dwelling on the past. He feared getting stuck in the negativity and jeopardizing his sobriety. He remembered as a child being punished severely when he lost his temper. His anger upset his mother and only made things worse.

Fortunately facing past anger in treatment is not a long-term process but it can bring about long-term relief. Therapists have a variety of techniques to help clients to feel and let go of anger. It is not an intellectual process, however, and many people who do not have any awareness of being angry will be able to release their rage with ease in a therapy setting. Others are blocked by fears of losing control, being abused further, hurting others or being shamed for expressing their anger.

Many therapists are trained to address these obstacles, particularly in group therapy. Although some individuals may try to fake anger to please a therapist, no relief will be felt this way. The skilled therapist is trained to know the difference. In the proper setting, given time and gentle support, most will be able to scream, rage and even feel good about it. No confrontation is necessary for this to occur. Done properly, rage release will feel extremely healing and energizing.

Once old anger or rage is released, the real work begins. In long-term therapy, with the support of healthy 12-Step groups, we must learn how to express our anger in the present and prevent the same buildup of pain in the future. With re-education (sometimes referred to as reparenting), we need to examine what we believe and expect of others, to reduce the number of things we get angry about.

Joseph expressed a good deal of his rage during the first few months of his treatment. Now he felt much less obsessed with his work and was receiving feedback from others that he seemed genuinely calm and less angry. He had a long way to go but he was out of his old rut and trying new ways of doing things.

Grief: Releasing The Hurt

The awareness and deepfelt pain of losses of childhood and adult life constitute feelings of grief. For Joseph and others like him, the losses may include the following:

- Realizing that he never had a childhood, never had a dad or mom who could love him.
- Remembering sadly the death of his favorite grandmother, whom he was not allowed to grieve.
- Feeling the isolation and deep sense of loneliness that was so ever-present that it had become invisible.
- Feeling the past and present estrangement from siblings who were so near but unavailable.
- Feeling the hurts of years of abuse, the tears not cried.
- Feeling despair when recalling the unfulfilled dreams of childhood for a happy life ahead.
- Looking at his children and seeing the same legacy for them, feeling helpless to change it.
- The abandonment of a lifetime of being with people and yet being alone.

This list only partially captures the intense anguish and despair felt when we truly let go and allow ourselves to experience it. We fear that once it is unleashed, it will never stop. We had very good reasons for avoiding feelings of grief. It is a very painful process. Many co-dependents have had years of depression and know sadness too well. Healthy grieving is quite different from that familiar "down" feeling. It has a thread of hope and a sense of healing.

In therapy Joseph did not feel his grief until he had discharged a great deal of anger. He had not cried since he was a child and had great difficulty letting his tears flow. He began grieving without tears in the loving support of other men in his therapy group. They understood and were not afraid of Joseph when he slowing became more vulnerable. When the tears finally came, they were truly the tears of a child. For the first few weeks Joseph felt out of control. He managed to work and function but his old defenses were not working well. He could not fake being OK, and his work did not serve as a distraction from all feeling.

Whenever he was alone, or in his support group, the feelings arose effortlessly. The sadness, loss and hurts were everywhere. For a few months Joseph was unable to support others, but asked them to be patient while he went through this painful time. Gradually the heaviness began to lift and he regained some control over where and when he would feel the pain. Memories had now become much clearer. He no longer ran from the feelings. In fact he felt himself changing internally, healing and becoming freer with each tear and expressed hurt.

Joseph's experience is fairly typical. Men and women have similar feelings but may express them differently. The pain can be compared to grief after the death of a significant person in one's life. While the length of time varies from person to person, the time period generally extends from an intense two to four months, followed by one to two years of gradual healing. The duration depends to some degree on the severity of the losses. If Joseph had been a Vietnam vet or an incest victim, for example, his grieving would require more time.

There is no right way to grieve but it is very important that you do it.

Fear

Unlike anger and grief, fear cannot be conquered through intense discharge. It is supported by a belief system, frequently by beliefs of a frightened, hurt little child within us. As children in a dysfunctional, abusive home, we may have very good reasons to be afraid. Experience has taught the child that the world is not a safe place. When we took risks, expressed a feeling, did something unpopular, the consequences in the family — and occasionally outside of the family — were very painful.

Some of our fears may be well founded, others are irrational and based on old beliefs from a child's perspective. Examples of fears expressed by co-dependents in treatment are:

- If you knew me, you would leave me.
- Anger kills people.
- No one can be trusted, especially not authority.
- If I make a mistake, you will think I'm bad.
- I know you will hurt me eventually.
- If I'm vulnerable, I will be hurt.
- I'll die if I'm alone (for a child, *alone* means death).

Another source of fear is our parents themselves. We can internalize fear that actually belongs to them, or our parents may teach fear by example and reinforce it in us.

When Joseph was little, his parents, who themselves had many disappointments in life, cautioned him against doing anything that might lead to failure or even embarrassment. Whenever he shared an idea or dream, their reaction was, "That is too hard for you, aim lower and you won't get hurt." If he expressed his fear outwardly, they reacted by shaming him and reminding him that "Big boys shouldn't let anyone know they are scared."

Joseph found that if he didn't take many risks and tried to look tough and aggressive, people didn't see his fear. Eventually he didn't feel it either. Becoming a counselor was a risk. Joseph feared failure so much that he caused himself to fail by believing he would.

A child may have a parent who is so fearful that he or she becomes smothering and overprotective. Although it may appear to be loving concern for the welfare of the child, it is more often the result of the parent's fears projected onto the child. When Nancy began her recovery she had many fears to overcome. She was afraid of crowds, afraid to drive in the city, afraid of high places, escalators, bridges, flying and many more. Her life was limited but she had grown so accustomed to adapting to her fears that she was not disturbed by it until she was with healthier people in a 12-Step group.

In order to change it was necessary for Nancy to separate her mother's fears from her own. She determined through facing each fear whether she felt afraid or had been taught to be afraid of it. In reality Nancy's greatest fear was of abandonment. She grew up protecting a mother who was mentally ill. Her mother's anxiety felt to Nancy as a young child as if her mother was abandoning her. To make her mother feel more secure Nancy did not take risks that were upsetting to her mother. Through reinforcement these fears gradually became her own.

In long-term treatment there are many moments when fear can be overwhelming. We may want to turn back, away from the painful feelings to our comfortable friend, denial. A supportive therapist, a nurturing group and the loving friends in a 12-Step support system are essential to helping us go on. The expression "Feel the fear and do it anyway!" serves as an excellent guide. Putting one foot in front of the other, looking ahead to those who have survived this process before you, and staying in the moment as much as possible are our best tools.

Another very useful saying, especially for perfectionists, is "trust the process." Many of us hate to feel vulnerable and out of control. We want to get There (whatever that means) in a hurry. We need frequent reminders that growth takes time and that with pain comes change and progress. If we rush the process to avoid the pain, we are right back where we began.

Shame

There are two sources of shame for children in painful families. The first is personal shame based on inner beliefs about oneself. The second is the shame learned from parents, which may be generations old.

The first is a direct result of being loved with conditions. Parents can only love children as much and as well as they love themselves. As infants and young children we must stay connected to a caregiver in order to survive. Since parents in a dysfunctional family are in emotional pain, it is much more difficult to connect, and any connection is very inconsistent and unpredictable.

Children discover at a very young age that certain behaviors work better than others to maintain an emotional connection with parents. They may learn that the world cannot be trusted, and it is wise not to be spontaneous and genuine in dealings with adults and even siblings. Without conscious awareness, children develop a pseudo-self or pretend self. They may feel ashamed of the "real" person within and believe they must hide in order to prevent abandonment.

Learned shame, passed on from one generation to the next, is also caused by secrets. Tanya discovered at the age of 42 that her mother and grandmother had both been victims of incest. Tanya herself had not been sexually abused, but was questioned at length by her therapist about the possibility because of the shame that she carried. She identified with other incest survivors in her group and began to wonder if she had repressed the memory of sexual abuse.

When Tanya's mother finally told her about the incest, Tanya began to understand many of her feelings about herself, which she could not attribute to direct abuse.

Tanya's mother had had great difficulty connecting with her daughter as a child. She was distant and superficial, avoiding eye contact and touch. Her mother became even more distant as Tanya entered puberty, seeming suspicious and untrusting of Tanya's physical and emotional growth. Tanya learned in time that much of the deep shame she was feeling was that projected onto her by her mother. When her mother looked at Tanya, she saw herself, the incest victim whom she treated with self-hate and shame. Keeping the secret for so many years had caused the shame to grow.

Treatment for shame is very different from the other feelings. It is a five- to eight-year (maybe even a lifetime) process. Shame is not discharged like anger; it is a wound that heals. The best of therapists can only give us opportunities to try out new beliefs about ourselves and to find those who will love us no matter who we are. In recovery we test over and over our belief that if we are known we will be abandoned. The first test is with a therapist or perhaps our first sponsor.

Here we expose some of our flaws and find that others have them too. Not only do they not leave but they want us to stay around. A therapy group is an excellent place to practice being real, angry, inappropriate or silly and experience the consequences. Long after therapy is over the work continues — both in 12-Step support groups and in one's closest relationships. The goal is never to arrive but to become increasingly congruent, that is, to appear on the outside as you feel on the inside — to give up the pseudo-self. For this it is essential that we consciously surround ourselves with a supportive network of people who want to know the real person inside.

Stage III: Understanding Letting Go And Forgiving

The stages of identification and expression of pain are never truly completed. Thus the shift to a stage of understanding, letting go and forgiving may be simultaneous with Stages I and II. A dramatic change in belief systems and even in behavior will be apparent once you release painful feelings.

During this third stage you will spend more time working on changing your thinking and behaving. If you have not expressed past emotional pain, it will be very difficult to move into this stage. Relapse into compulsive behavior or stress-related illness are the cues that you have more feelings work to do. Remember that you won't ever get perfect. This is an ongoing process.

Although it is definitely hard work to make permanent changes in the way we live, this stage is much less painful than the previous two. Denial is lessened and we no longer have pain to medicate. Change, then, is a matter of learning and practicing new ways of living. This is a stage of thinking and doing as well as feeling. For everything we let go of there is something new and better to replace it. There are losses and new beginnings. This stage is more about living than about recovery. Using a support system helps to prevent backsliding and reminds us about who we once were and who we would like to become.

Understanding

Once you have experienced and taken responsibility for your own pain, you will reach a point where you are at peace within yourself about how you arrived here. There is no need to resent or focus on your family as the source of your problems. You now realize that you are a small part of a multigenerational family system where no one made a choice to be dysfunctional, and very few people had their needs met.

The recovering person in this third stage feels a new connection to their history and may feel humbled and blessed to have had the rare opportunity of recovery. With it comes an increasing sense of awe in this process and gratitude for what has been learned and gained from the pain of the past. There is a strong belief that we can change anything we desire to change about who we are today, but there is no need to focus on the past any longer.

Letting Go

Letting go encompasses the following:

- We no longer try to change others, or if we do, we quickly realize the futility of it.
- We let go of blame and anger that are part of a victim role we no longer need to play.
- We gradually begin to enjoy being "out of control," while we learn to use our personal and spiritual power.
- We place others, including our children, in the hands of a Higher Power, while we strive to be as healthy in our relating to them as we can be at this point in our lives.
- We let go of the future, striving to live in the moment, looking ahead to plan our actions but not the outcomes or feelings.
- We slowly let go of fantasies about how things should have been and begin to live and accept the way things are.

Forgiveness Of Self And Others

Amends are made as we undo old hurts by being the best self we can be today. It is a necessary step since there is no victim of abuse who has not also been an abuser. Sometimes saying "I'm sorry" will make a difference. But more often we must prove over time that we can be trusted and that we really have changed. The best thing we can do for others is to be the healthiest person we know how to be, treating others as we would like to be treated no matter what their reaction.

Amends to oneself often are called "self-caring." This term is more accurate than the word selfish because it implies self-responsibility as a priority in one's life. Victims hold others responsible. In this stage of recovery we take an honest look at the way we've been treating ourselves and we try to become our own best friend. This may include physical care, getting dental checkups or quitting smoking, and certainly includes emotional and spiritual care. We put ourselves in loving places and support the child within as a loving parent would.

Parenting our children requires both that we be our best self and take an active role in learning how to support another life while we do it. It is a serious responsibility in later stages of recovery. The next chapter will address this specifically.

Building A Strong Support System For Life

Doing life requires a lot of help. I often hear from recovering people the faulty assumption that "normal" healthy people don't need the same support as recovering people. They have come to believe that safety is limited to AA, Al-Anon or another 12-Step group. Every human being needs support and most healthy individuals have found it one way or another without calling it recovery. Late-stage recovery is a time to join the world, not to find a cocoon to hide in. We do not need treatment, self-help books and conferences forever.

Just because a person doesn't know the meaning of the word co-dependency does not mean they have nothing in common with us or that we can't relate. Family members, spouse or lover, lifetime friends, church, spiritual guides — all have an important role in making up a solid but ever-changing support system.

For those who are single, without a primary committed relationship, life remains full but the possibility of a future partner is never ruled out. What you believe is what you get. Surround yourself with those who affirm possibility, whether financial, emotional or physical. The quality of your support system is a direct reflection of how you see yourself right now.

Bringing Humor Into Life

As we move away from pain we don't need to go to a comedy club to laugh or smile. Laughter is everywhere we choose to find it. Smiling is a genuine expression of the joy we feel internally. Stressful situations and serious problems have a funny side to them. We prefer to associate with those who will help us to see that humor in life.

Play, whether formal or just a spontaneous response to life in general, takes on an important role, as it balances our work and personal lives. The child within is ever present, teasing, giggling, and enjoying the absurdity of life. No matter how bleak the situation, there is room for a moment of humor.

Finding The Right Guides For Your Journey

There are many ways to recover and many people and places to help you along the way. Rule number one is to go where you feel safe and connected. There is no right way despite what many professionals believe. It doesn't matter where you begin. In fact many individuals have actually begun recovery long before they are consciously aware of it. Reading and seeking new ideas and information is one way to remain noncommittal while testing the waters. Perfectionists may tend to stay here a bit too long. We want to make sure we know everything before we take any chances!

Self-help 12-Step groups are definitely a great place to start. Free of charge and with anonymity you will receive support and guidance from others who understand. The following is a list of things to look for — based on the experience of myself and others who have learned the hard way — when you seek professional help.

    1. Reputation based on long-term experience is the best reference a therapist or program can offer. New doesn't

mean bad; but it may be safer to listen to friends who are familiar with the quality of the service.

2. A therapist does not need to be recovering or even an expert on co-dependency to be good. It is more important that he or she is an open, honest, real human being who can identify with your struggles but is not in them at the moment. Too much or too little identification can be a problem.

3. Support and encouragement for 12-Step involvement in addition to counseling is important from a therapist.

4. Look for long-term care rather than short-term problem solving. In inpatient treatment, length of program is less important than length of outpatient followup. Expect up to two years for the average person, longer for those with severe abuse or complications.

5. A nurturing approach is much more effective than a confrontive approach.

6. Active, even directive therapy is preferred over the passive, psychoanalytic approach. In the beginning you may need some specific guidance and suggestions, somewhat like parenting. This should lessen with time and your ability to handle it. The goal is to work hard and become able to apply what you learn to your life, not to sit and have it done to you.

7. Group therapy will move you faster. If at all possible, it should be included in your treatment plan at some point. Same-sex groups are extremely helpful, especially for men. Neither is essential, just a strong suggestion.

8. Credentials are important but slightly less important than the issues above. Be certain the therapist has enough training and recovery (if applicable) to be helping you. Training in this field may or may not mean degrees. Ask how long he or she has been doing the kind of counseling you are looking for, and where he or she was trained. Talk to others who are seeing this therapist.

9. There is a time in treatment when experiential work such as role play, sculpture or psychodrama can be very helpful in raising feelings. If your therapist does

not do this kind of work, it may be wise to utilize an inpatient treatment program as an adjunct to your out-patient counseling.

10. Take responsibility for your own process. Do not become a victim in therapy. You are there by choice and you have the right to leave at any time. You can decide when and where to take risks. There are no gurus to save you or make you well. No program can save you or make you sick. You can think and feel at the same time. Take very good care of yourself. You are important!

6

Imperfect But Healthy Parenting: What Is A Healthy Family Anyway?

I must begin by saying there is nothing magical about creating a healthy family. We are born with every tool necessary to do it. Many of us, however, developed some new tools in order to survive, and these became stronger over time and through repeated exercise. Our healthy skills, atrophied or weakened through lack of use, simply need to be redeveloped. I believe this is true for all of us, even the most damaged.

The first requirement is to get the treatment we need and begin personal healing before we attempt to give it away to anyone else. The good news is that underneath all the pain and learned dysfunctional patterns is a person who is basically loving, has common sense and wants to connect with others. You can learn a new way of doing things much faster than it took you to learn the damaging ways.

There is no point in time at which we can certify a family as
healthy. Most of us fluctuate between health and dysfunction as
we are affected by changing conditions in our lives. The key is
really in awareness of the goal, what we are striving toward,
knowing we will never arrive. When we can accept our own
humanness and that of others, we can relax and enjoy the ride.

When we ride on a roller coaster, we can either open our
eyes and love the excitement of it, feeling alive and exhila-
rated, or we can close our eyes and wait for it to be over with
the least amount of distress possible. Which will you choose?
I plan to enjoy the ride!

When we board the roller coaster at an amusement park,
we assume that it has been thoroughly inspected for safety
and we make a conscious decision to trust despite what it
looks like. Relationships are like this too. It is up to the adults
in the family to inspect and maintain the integrity of the
system to be sure that it is safe for everyone. For this reason
I would like to address the issue of healthy couples before
discussing family.

Healthy Coupling

Relationships: Can't live with them, can't live without
them. Most of us would agree with the confusion that results
from getting close to another person. Perfectionists want to
take the risk out of relationships by controlling all variables.
Unfortunately this takes the fun out of it. Intimacy can be
pretty exciting and pretty terrifying all at the same time. Let's
assume that you have worked through the pain with a process similar to what I described in the previous chapter. You
are now ready to teach people how to treat you by showing
them how you treat yourself.

Interdependence

Partners in a healthy relationship feel safe and supported.
There is an agreement between the parties to be there for
each other to the best of their ability on a consistent basis.
This does not imply perfection. We all have off days when we
cannot be there for anyone. In an intimate, committed rela-

tionship there is an understanding that we will be each other's best friend — but not each other's *only* friend.

Interdependence means that we can rely on one another without assuming the problems or feelings of the other person. It is a tricky balance to learn to hold onto yourself while you give to another. In dependent relationships we expect the other to suffer with us and in the end we wind up with two dysfunctional people instead of one. I can support you and love you and still have a life of my own in an interdependent relationship.

There will be times when we are going in opposite directions and rely more on support from outside than within our relationship. The perfectionist in us may occasionally demand, "You be there whenever I ask, but I cannot do the same for you." Implicit in interdependence is the understanding that this is not a constant, perfect support. Resentment and hurt may result when we are needy and feel unsupported by a partner. Healthy people have enough self-worth and personal security to not feel destroyed and abandoned with the fluctuations in a relationship. They express the hurt and move on.

Intimacy

Intimacy is the glue of a relationship. It is the reason we are together, a basic human need. It is the emotional connection described in chapter 4. Intimacy is also a flowing, changing process. We cannot simply make a decision to be intimate and then do it. Assuming we have the ingredients mentioned earlier — identity, willingness to face rejection, ability to share feelings, clear boundaries and interdependence — we need to make sure we include the following elements in order to maintain an intimate connection:

- Time spent together away from children and friends.
- Shared secrets, whether humorous stories or painful history, mean greater risks are taken with each other than with anyone else.
- Space between you as you need it. Private interests, personal belongings, physical space that is yours. It makes the coming together more meaningful.

- Nonsexual physical contact that is spontaneous, not ritual, includes eye contact, touch, affection and so on.
- A desire to know one another and to help the other grow in whatever direction he or she desires.
- Fun with others gives us a chance to know another aspect of each other and brings balance into our expectations of the relationship.

Growing And Changing Sexuality

Sexuality is not a constant. If we wish to have a healthy sexual relationship we must also learn to enjoy and adjust with the changes and growth in ourselves and our partners. Men and women are not the same. This is a fact that a healthy person with good self-esteem knows and enjoys. Partners in a homosexual relationship also understand and take pleasure in the uniqueness of their partner. Relationships would have little energy or attraction if we both had identical sexual needs.

When we have a strong personal identity, we feel more secure in developing a clear sexual identity. The person I am today is just that: the person I am today. Many variables affect how we relate sexually on any given day. Examples are physical well-being; stress; frequency of intercourse; level of intimacy in the relationship in recent days and hours; unexpressed anger or resentment; worries about children, environment or privacy; partner's needs or expectations. This is not something we can control, predict, schedule or do perfectly. The longer we are together the more affected we may be by these variables.

During the infatuation stage at the beginning of a relationship, we are "blissfully blind" and tend to tune out any distraction. This also changes in time. The beauty of a long-term relationship is the security and safety we feel once the excitement has lessened. We can take greater risks with a person we truly know and trust. The sexual relationship becomes an expression of intimacy rather than simply a physical exercise in mutual gratification. Intimacy precedes good sex. Of course it is possible to be satisfied occasionally without an emotional connection, but it does not contribute to the health of the relationship.

Healthy couples do not expect or need to be in sync with each encounter, but take pleasure in the pleasure of the other. It is again interdependence, in that we both gain something and we both give something, but not necessarily at the same time or in equal proportions. We are each ultimately responsible for our own sexuality, communicating needs and changes in what we desire. We should not expect our partner to read our mind. As in any healthy communication, healthy couples stay current with their feelings.

Communication

Perfectionists have a great deal of difficulty with communication because the goal is to gain control and to be proven right. Healthy communication is without an agenda, knowing that the process of sharing will accomplish more than you could deliberately set out to do. You cannot assume that you are either good at it or you are not. It is a skill that must be developed through determination and practice, but one person cannot do it alone.

Within the relationship, time and setting often will influence the quality of communication. For example, we may think that driving to work and back is a good opportunity to share. The car, unfortunately, is a very poor setting. We cannot have eye contact or observe body language to understand our partner. It is work to make the time for such important interaction. We need daily opportunities for sharing feelings about responsibilities, job and children. And we also need more private opportunities, when we are not exhausted, to talk about more intimate subjects such as sex, feelings about each other and so on. Staying current prevents the buildup of resentments or the pain of misunderstandings.

A much neglected area of communication is listening. When we are afraid or threatened, we tend to block our ability to hear so we can prepare our defense. Listening requires total availability, visual and physical. We all know how poorly we listen while we're watching television or cleaning the house. Since relationships most often fail due to poor communication, this needs to be kept a priority.

Life Outside Of The Relationship

Occasionally we may slide back into the comfort of having one person to turn to who does not require a phone call or special plans. It is very easy to rely only on your partner for conversation, fun, moral support or just diversion. This is a sure way to destroy a good thing.

Healthy relationships balance the time spent with each other and with friends. I believe the emphasis is best put on time together, so that there is adequate opportunity for healthy communication. A support system should not take us away from family and the important relationships in our lives, but can make it easier to have healthy relationships.

Same-sex friends are very important. Our sisterhood and brotherhood needs to be preserved to help strengthen identity. Opposite-sex friends help us to gain perspective on how the other half feels and lives.

Time with extended family does not always have to be spent as a couple. We can have special times, even an occasional holiday, with siblings or parents without our partner's involvement. Our partner does not necessarily like or enjoy the company of the families or friends. That is perfectly OK.

The Rewards Of Healthy Relationships

These are some of the major ingredients in healthy coupling. Becoming a family with children is an awesome but enjoyable and rewarding experience for healthy couples. Since healthy couples, even recovering couples, are making choices instead of reacting to life, everything takes on new meaning. Each is responsible for the quality of his or her life, which is lived one day at a time in process.

Being part of a functional family can provide many positive things.

- Physical safety and greater financial security through shared space and resources.
- The joy of being around children and letting your inner child out in the process.

- The opportunity to heal painful wounds of the past while starting over in your own family.
- Emotional support and stability from being surrounded with people who know you and love you no matter what, and don't require long explanations of who you are.
- Parent/child bonding, which is an indescribable inner experience.
- Shared spirituality, relying together on a Higher Power to protect and guide. Spirituality grows in groups.
- A home that is a haven, the safest place in the world, where you can let down your guard and just be.

We are all capable of bringing this into our lives, and we all deserve it. It is what we were meant to do with each other: love and be loved. Now how do we do it?

It certainly has nothing to do with looking good or doing it right. The greatest skill we need to develop is our own ability to tune in to our instincts or our internal spirit for answers to difficult questions.

Reading books, particularly about child development, can be very helpful. But at some point you put down the books, sit by yourself and just do it. You will have what you need when you need it. Perfectionists, before having children, catastrophize it by thinking they must know everything before a child is conceived. This is a matter of trusting the process.

Three simple rules to follow may serve us well:

1. Be what you want everyone else to be.
2. Make feelings important.
3. Respect adults and children.

What Is A Healthy Family Anyway?

I gathered the following information by asking this question of recovering people all over the county, "What is a healthy family?" You will see from the answers that we really *do* know how to do it. Remember: The qualities discussed below are an ideal to aim for, not a goal to achieve.

Parenting Is A Priority

Adults who choose to be parents do so knowing the responsibility they are assuming and make it important. They develop a balance between having a life as an adult and putting children ahead of many other things that would be important if they were not parents. Parenting means sacrifice by choice, not as a victim.

It means knowing what you don't know and finding out. It means acknowledging your limitations due to family background, and owning them. It means sharing fully in this task with another parent, if possible, and in some cases putting aside negative feelings for that parent for the benefit of a child. As a single parent it may mean keeping to yourself the painful truths about their dad or mom, letting children discover for themselves what is real.

It means playing when you don't really want to; putting your exhaustion and heartaches aside until you aren't needed; watching children and being sensitive to the needs they cannot verbalize. A healthy parent seeks out the child who has become quiet or rebellious to find out what's really going on inside.

As parents we get to relive our childhoods and have the opportunity to feel our old hurts and joys and share them. We often will need to hold our pain until children are asleep or away from us before we let the tears flow. We may not be able to talk on the phone anytime we want or go to our favorite restaurants since children may not like them. We may have to wait to make time for those things we need while we balance the needs of our adult relationships at the same time.

We will need to stop often and long to see the beauty of our children and feel the immense love we give and receive, because there is no assurance of getting anything back. They owe us nothing and will not ever be as grateful as we'd like. Until they are parents, and maybe not even then, they will not know what we did for them.

And to this we make a lifetime commitment and can't imagine life without it!

There Is A "Do Talk" Rule

It is a given in a healthy, functioning family that talking helps. Since you will not be shamed or abused for having a problem or a painful feeling or even joy, it is safe to share. When children or adults share, they may ask for advice, a hug or just a listening ear. It is not assumed that you need to be fixed just because you have a problem. Because it is so easy and feels so good, you do it often.

Talking may be about details of one's day, sharing lives, exchanging stories so that we can know each other and watch each other grow, or it may be about feelings. Parents not only encourage sharing, but model it so that children learn healthy ways of expressing themselves. Time is set aside to create opportunities for sharing, both as a whole family and as individuals. This does not take much effort, since family members like each other and want to spend time together.

As children go through stages of separation, as in adolescence, they need to share less with parents and more with peers. When parents are secure and have an intact relationship themselves, this is viewed as healthy and normal. This is a time when a parent is on standby status, remaining available and interested without forcing communication. In this way the child can come and go emotionally without feeling like they are abandoning the parent, and the parent can begin to let go of the role of protector a bit.

Feelings Are Appropriately Expressed

Healthy expression of feelings within a family requires first that parents know how to do it, and second that they do so frequently. Children see how it's done and imitate. Parents may guide children by setting limits and teaching new skills as needed, but parents at least try to learn these things before they "preach" it to their children. Anger is the most difficult feeling to contend with in parenting. Although we all agree that children ought to express anger, none of us is comfortable in hearing it.

The boundaries and limits set by parents protect not only the children but also the adults from the damage of abuse. In healthy families children know what the limits are. For example, you cannot call Mom and Dad names, hit people or destroy property. The specific limits in each home will be very different, determined by the values of parents and the special needs of children. There is no rule book for this but there are a few absolutes:

- In a healthy family it will not be OK to abuse, verbally or physically, no matter what the situation.
- Long periods of angry silence will be confronted.
- Respect will be shown in the form of attentive listening, persistence by parents in trying to understand and putting in the time it takes to do it.
- Parents will not expect maturity and logic from a child who is not developmentally able to demonstrate it.
- Children will respect parents, but not rigidly and perfectly. They will "lose it" at times and still be loved, since what they are doing is very normal.
- When children share painful feelings — fears, loneliness or hurts — healthy parents do not overreact, nor do they shame or minimize. They accept this as normal and listen.
- Tears and sadness are allowed and healthy parents are able to support and remain available until children are ready to share.
- There is no need to fix a problem immediately; but when consistent patterns appear, they will attempt to find the cause and correct the problem or get help as necessary.
- Professional help will be viewed as a useful tool whenever the family is stuck or needs extra support. It is not postponed until problems become severe.

When parents themselves are hurting, they depend first on each other and then on their outside supports, seeking professional help as they need it. They inform children in an age-appropriate way that something is wrong. They neither depend on children nor pretend nothing is wrong.

For example, a father who has just lost his job knows that telling his children what happened is very important, but reassuring them that he knows what to do about it is also important. Children worry and have fears when they see a parent struggling. The healthy parent can take care of himself or herself, while also attending to the needs of the child. We may not be as effective with our children when we are hurting, but they will not be ignored. In this way parents can model to the child that talking helps, that no one has to do it alone and that problems can be solved in time.

There Are Visible Signs Of Health

The healthy family does not have to look good in the social sense, with the best clothes, perfectly behaved children and so on. But there will be observable signs of the good feelings in a family:

- Eye contact. Family members look directly at each other when they talk.
- Smiles will not be constant but you will sense that these people like each other.
- Touch, in the form of gentle and appropriate physical contact, along with a softness of posture, makes them look relaxed in receiving a touch.
- Humor and laughter at times (not teasing or sarcasm), showing a positive outlook and a shared humorous view of the world.
- Openness and comfort with each other, demonstrated through attentive listening or even comfort with silence.

Every family goes through bad times when communication shuts down or people don't feel safe. This must be seen as a dynamic process, not a fixed way of being. In family therapy it becomes clear in a moment when the healthy factors above are present. Even when a healthy family is in crisis, some of those things listed will remain. What shines through it all is their love for each other, both felt and expressed.

Stress Is Expected And Prepared For

Since crisis is not needed for distraction, it is not well toler-
ated in a healthy family. Parents model for children how to see
a problem coming and to prevent it if possible. They demonstrate planning ahead, seeking out necessary information,
checking out alternatives, disagreeing and negotiating and
attempting to solve what can be solved.

Healthy parents believe that although life has its difficulties,
it is not a constant struggle. It will never be perfect and doesn't
need to be, but we need to maintain enough calm to enjoy
the good things as well. Parents are able to see past the crisis.
They continue to live and attend to important things like
parenting while they address the problem.

In a healthy marriage couples are able to work together on
a crisis. The may disagree about solutions but will have a
common goal of resolution. They will not use this as a means
to scapegoat one another or to distract from other more serious problems. When things have been chaotic or stressful,
sometimes even due to good things like a vacation or moving
to a new house, parents may restore order through return to
routine, structure and predictability. Children feel secure knowing someone is in charge and taking control of the situation.

Looking Good families often appear to be very active. Parents take children to lessons and sports activities every night
of the week, believing this is the best thing for children.
Children and parents also need structured family time and
frequent quiet in order to have intimacy and opportunities to
feel and share feelings. A busy family can be a very stressed-
out family. Healthy families may not need as much activity,
since they enjoy home and special moments with each other.

There Is An Absence Of Extremes

Moderation and balance are reflected in both positive and
negative aspects of the family. No one looks perfect or totally
dysfunctional. They are a cross between television's Huxtable
family and *Roseanne.* There will be flexibility. Family
members will have different ways of doing things and dif-

fering opinions. Not everyone will dress the same way or share the same interests.

When they find something they like to do, a sport for example, they will do it moderately. They won't invest all their spare time and money, insisting that all the children love it. If there is something they feel strongly about, they are able to care without becoming obsessed with it to the exclusion of things like intimacy and fun. Rather than believing in rights and wrongs, they try to see the grey area. This also applies to their religious and political beliefs.

Since they are feeling more secure and less fearful of change than most, they are constantly growing and changing as they learn new things and have greater opportunities. This behavior is modeled by parents for children, and encouraged as a way of life. As in the other conditions described, this is not done with perfection. Everyone gets extreme at times, especially when we are under stress or feeling fearful. Many people in recovery comment about enjoying the boredom of a much less intense lifestyle. Sometimes, if we have been used to a lot of stress, we just need to stir it up with a little excitement once in a while!

Disagreements And Differences Of Opinion Occur

When individuals in a family have strong personal identities, they frequently will clash. The same happens when children grow up and go out into the world with other adults. The best place to learn how to handle conflict in an effective way is at home. Once again, the responsibility falls with parents to model this skill. Not only will they have conflicts with each other, but life gives us many opportunities to face others with our anger and differing opinions.

A healthy family is not necessarily a quiet one. It is OK to fight, but skills of fair fighting are taught. They might include such lessons as:

- Assertive communication. Explaining how you feel rather than blaming; knowing what you think and what you want but being open to compromise.

- Win-Win. How to get what I want and what you want.
- Expressing anger with respect.
- Hanging in there when you want to run or slam the door.
- Taking time out and coming back to resolve, knowing when to give the other person some space.
- Gaining resolution, not giving up and just forgetting it.
- How to let go when the answer is no.

Parents can do this with children. Jeanne Illsley-Clarke and Connie Dawson, in their book *Growing Up Again*, use the term "creative hassling," which gives a very positive focus to the disagreements between parents and children. There is so much to be learned from expressing ourselves openly and listening to our children do the same.

Parents also can model how to argue with the salesperson who overcharged them or the mechanic who has not yet fixed their car. Healthy adults do not avoid these difficult conflicts, and they do not bully or overpower others.

The Family System Is Open To Outside Support

A healthy family is an open, dynamic system, growing and changing with the years. A support system exists for the individuals in the family in the form of friends, school groups, and so on, and also for the family as a group. Church, recovery groups, neighborhood, extended family (grandparents, aunts, uncles, cousins) and old family friends all serve as support for the health of the family. People come and go, children may have preferences and dislikes for some, but the overall security that comes from knowing you are not alone is very important.

There are times when it feels that home is not a safe place. At those times a support system carries us. During periods of financial stress or health problems, they may literally support the family. People who do not have extended family support need to seek out this type of unconditional love from others. In the hard times it may be the only assurance that we will be OK.

No family is an island!

Remember too that since health means balance and lack of extremes, the healthy family is not without privacy as well.

Parenting Means Guiding And Letting Go

Parenting is a gradual, continuous process of letting go from birth to adulthood. Initially parents are totally responsible for chidren, later they serve only as occasional guides. It is the duty of parents to protect children while they grow into the beautiful people they were supposed to be. Healthy parents do not have an agenda of expectations for their children. "Perfect" parenting would assume that the parent knows exactly what a child needs at all times.

Discipline is aimed at protecting the child, not the parent. It addresses behavior, not the worth of the child. It uses natural or logical consequences so that the child learns to self-correct rather than look to others for approval or disapproval.

Healthy parents try to get out of the middle in guiding the behavior of their children. Punishment eventually becomes a battle of wills between parent and child; healthy discipline becomes the means by which a child learns what works best for him or her to get the desired results. Not only will parents be pleased by the child's good behavior, the child will learn to develop internal motivation to behave well.

Children are respected for being able to say no. Parents may have concerns about what a child says no to, but overall it is a good skill to have. Saying no to green beans today may mean saying no to cocaine in 12 years. The parent who can support the process while addressing areas of disagreement one at a time will have a healthier child. Many times saying no is really the child's need to say to a parent "I am *me*, I am not you!" Parents who are themselves secure and have a strong identity view this as a positive skill.

Limit-setting is the responsibility of healthy parents. The limits are like an invisible defense around children, protecting them until they are ready to stretch further. A two-year-old needs a very small space to operate in and a 15-year-old needs a very big space. But neither has the ability to handle total freedom into the world. Healthy discipline provides this limit in the form of family rules and structure, not in the form of punishment. Instead of punishment there are consequences that make sense and fit the mistake.

Children are supposed to make lots of mistakes. The more they make while they are children, the less they will need to make as adults. Experience is growth.

Affirmation And Praise Work Together

Praise is a nice way to help children and adults to feel motivated to do well. It is important in the development of achievers — children who get good grades and who seek excellence in what they do. Healthy families balance praise with affirming the worth and value of the person. It is more important that you feel good about yourself and know that you are loved, than that parents applaud your accomplishments.

Affirmation comes in the form of verbal and nonverbal support for your existence, while praise supports what you do. Nonverbal affirmation is a simple touch, hearing your name, eye contact, a special attentive "Hello" from a parent, smiles for no reason. Verbal affirmations are validating comments such as: "I like to be with you, You're so special to me, I love you no matter what you do." On this topic I strongly recommend reading Jeanne Illsley-Clarke's *Self-Esteem: A Family Affair* for more affirmations for adults and children.

I believe affirmation is necessary to raise children who have good self-esteem. Praise alone creates children who do a lot but don't enjoy it. A healthy family incorporates affirmation and praise into everyday living as naturally as breathing. Recovering families may begin with a more formalized approach until they learn this new skill, but eventually it becomes second nature to affirm others.

Living with affirmation creates positive self-talk in adults and children. Family members learn to say nice things to themselves, then grow up and pass it on to their children.

Parents Model Intimacy

A healthy relationship between parents is just as important to children as it is to the couple themselves. Children can only learn how to have a healthy relationship from watching the adults in their environment. In a single-parent family this needs to be shown through friendships or serious dating relationships. It is important for children in a single-parent situation to spend time with healthy couples. The single parent also can model what it is like to be alone by choice in a healthy way, which teaches another important skill.

In a healthy family parents practice what they preach. Children witness the specialness of the relationship and come to expect this same healthy bond when they grow up. They will know the difference betweeen sexual attraction and love. They will know when they are being treated badly, because they have seen respect and kindness.

Children have high self-esteem and begin to make choices in friendships based on the feelings they have about themselves. This is the beginning of learning to have a healthy relationship.

Divorce can occur even within a healthy family. This too can be done with health, although it will not be without pain. But respect, if not love, can be maintained between parents and a healthy parenting relationship continued. Divorce in and of itself does not damage children. The way we live prior to and during the divorce may. Healthy couples have a choice about how they go about it. This is not an easy task, and it will not be done perfectly.

Parents Are Open About Family History

Children in this family will know where they came from — the good, the bad and the ugly. Parents will share what they know about family history, if possible, recording information and pictures that tell the story. More important, there will be no secrets. Children will be told in age-appropriate doses about painful events in the lives of parents and grandparents, and also family stories that are humorous and interesting.

Information, such as alcoholism, suicide, cancer and divorce, has no emotional charge when shared at an early age with children. It is only when they believe it has been withheld, or if they sense your pain about it, that they will be disturbed.

A mother who has been an incest victim may share information with a three-year-old, such as, "Your body is your own, no one should touch you without your permission. Once when I was little I was touched in a way I didn't like but I didn't know I could say no. I didn't tell and that hurt me very much. I want you to say no. You can tell me if anyone hurts you, no matter what they say." As the child matures, the information could become more specific. Healthy parents want to prevent future pain for their children by being honest and open today.

Is there really a perfectly healthy family, as described in this chapter? No. We can't do it all, but we can keep trying. We'll do well in some areas and poorly in others. The goal is to keep on growing, accepting your limitations and being kind to yourself.

When these conditions begin to be present in the family, home becomes the haven it was intended to be. It is truly the safest place there is, where we know we can be ourselves and still be loved.

Beginning with your imperfect self is the only way to get closer to this ideal. We cannot give our children what we don't have, and creating a Looking Good imitation is not the answer. This contribution to yourself becomes a major contribution toward changing a family for generations to come. You are important!

7

Finding Balance
In Imperfection

This chapter is about balance. If you are still a perfectionist, you will be tempted to skip it as too frivolous, and not intense enough to keep your interest. But fun and imperfection go hand in hand, so *please* — read on.

Normally I would need to have any information for a chapter *perfectly* organized before beginning to write. For this chapter I am deliberately taking an enormous risk by jumping in without such fastidious preparation. I hope it will be therapeutic for all of us!

Imperfect Things To Do And Enjoy

Over the years I have brought some balance into my life by consciously hiring people who have a great sense of humor and are extreme risk takers — actually bordering on the bizarre a good share of the time. I have asked this group of experts on the "inappropriate" to assist in preparing a list of "Imperfect Things To Do And Enjoy." As perfectionists we will probably need such a written resource, since we tend to have difficulty coming up with creative, fun ideas on our own.

I have grouped them according to large-group, small-group and individual activities. Take what's useful and give the rest to your friends. (I assure you I will return to more intellectual information before this chapter ends.)

Large Group Activities

National Imperfection Day

Julie Ingram of the Caron staff offers this suggestion for use with a staff, recovery group or even a family reunion.

Everyone in the group is asked to write down two things about each of the others in the group that they tend to do perfectly on a consistent basis. For example: having perfect makeup, being perfectly organized, parenting perfectly. It is necessary for us to get the information about ourselves from others because we don't see ourselves as others see us.

Out of the complete list, the group chooses three items for each person, which he or she will then have to do imperfectly for National Imperfection Day. Julie cautions us about becoming too perfect about being imperfect at these three things!

An Adult Child Party

Julie Ingram suggests this activity for a family reunion — it does not require healthy participants! Before the party each guest is sent an invitation with the following instructions:

1. Everyone is allowed to be a child for the day. It is OK to relax and enjoy yourself.
2. Only casual clothes can be worn.
3. Each guest must send to the planning committee one game and one special food he or she liked as a child.

4. Any other ideas or suggestions will be welcomed and encouraged.

Games could include hide and seek, red light, duck-duck-goose, tag, water-gun battles, jump rope, jacks, hopscotch, badminton, bubbles and any other fun game.

Food might include hot dogs, hamburgers, chicken, peanut butter and jelly sandwiches, popcorn, chips, pretzels, home-made ice cream, candy, sodas, lemonade or any other food that brings the child out.

The party may be videotaped and a copy sent to each family. Party favors of balloons or toys may be given to each guest, and fire works would be a great ending!

The planner of this party should ask for help and have fun doing it.

Praise For Imperfection

In the workplace implement praise for imperfection as a policy.

The next time an employee, co-worker or boss makes a mistake, instead of shaming and criticizing do the following:

1. Let the person know that making a mistake is a minor event, the person is not a mistake.
2. Let the person know how important he or she is to you and to the workplace.
3. Don't criticize the person in front of other co-workers.
4. Encourage some kind of learning from the mistake.

By showing a positive attitude, employer and employee both will feel a lot happier. Respect and kindness are conta-gious and will encourage enthusiasm and excellence without any negative consequences.

A Mock Wedding

At one particularly stressful period for the staff of our Res-idential Co-dependency program, a group of therapists decided to have a mock wedding for two unattached staff members. We all spent weeks planning for the event, with costumes, props, music and even a written ceremony. I served as the justice of the peace but could not stop laughing long enough to do an efficient job.

We included several drunk relatives (only acting, of course), a former girlfriend of the groom (crying loudly throughout), a soloist singing "Oh Promise Me," all followed by a lovely cake and gifts. Naturally this all took place after patients had gone home, and gave the staff a chance for healing laughter and team togetherness.

The more stressful the workplace, the more necessary it is to let go once in a while.

Affirmations Competition

Scott Slattery contributed this idea: The Affirmations Committee of Caron Family Services (invented for this special purpose) orchestrated a week-long event for anyone wishing to participate. Their instructions were as follows:

"To those courageous, special, uniquely creative and genuinely sensitive competitors who wish to be a part of this inaugural event, the rules are rather simple and possibly even fun. If you choose to participate, your name will be (gently) dropped into a hat, and names will be randomly drawn and paired. Once names have been matched it will be up to each competitor in the pair to exchange one affirmation a day for the following week. The only rule is that every affirmation given must be improved upon by the next one given — *the one up rule!*

"For example, if person A says, 'I like your left shoe,' person B may say, 'I like *both* of your shoes.' (We all know that you cannot actually make an Affirmation worse, but competing is fun anyway!)"

By Friday the group was totally affirmed.

Crazy Sock Or Hat Day

Here's another suggestion from Scott: Ask in advance for everyone at your work setting, 12-Step group or wherever you spend a lot of time to join in making the day a little lighter by wearing a crazy hat or funny socks to work. Another variation is Bring a Toy (or stuffed animal) to Work Day.

II. Small-Group Or One-To-One

- Take a walk on a rainy day, stepping in puddles along the way.
- Play old music and dance without worrying about how you look.
- Rent the funniest movie you've ever seen and invite friends over for popcorn and laughs. (Don't clean the house first.)
- Go to children's movies or read children's books. We are making up for lost time here.
- Play crazy games for laughs, not competition.
- Share ridiculous jokes such as this one contributed by Cindy Zollman of our staff, who heard it from ACoAs in treatment:

Two ACoAs are out duck hunting with their dog. They've been at it all day to no avail. The one guy looks at the other guy and asks, "What are we doing wrong?" The other guy looks back and says, "Why don't you try throwing the dog higher?"

III. Imperfect Activities To Do For Yourself

- Keep wind-up toys in your office. I also have a pig collection there.
- Keep a jar full of nurturing fun things you love to do on little slips of paper. Examples: Taking a bubble bath, shooting a basketball at the playground, riding your bike, playing jacks, reading, listening to a particular tape. Pick one whenever you're feeling needy and definitely include these on your Saturday "To Do" list.
- Swing on the swings at the playground.
- Post affirmations you need where you will see them easily — the bathroom mirror, the kitchen cupboard,

the car, and so on. Move them and change them often so they don't become invisible.

- Deliberately leave something undone every day. At the end of the day reflect with pride on how well you let go of it.
- On Saturday make a list of things you have no intention of doing and *don't do them!*
- Be very quiet several times a day, especially when you are too busy. Answers will come, priorities will get clearer.
- Simplify. This one requires explanation. Simplify can mean cleaning your attic and getting rid of the clutter in your life. The less you have, the less you need to keep track of. It also means don't buy what you don't need. Hire others to do things you don't like to do. You'd be amazed at how inexpensive housekeeping is and how good you feel when you aren't doing it all. (Or just get someone to do the ironing!)

   It also may be about settling for less than excellence in things that don't matter, leaving more energy for what does matter.

- Stop and build fun into your day. Even while writing this book, I planned each day for something distracting to do in the middle of it, whenever I needed — a puzzle to work on, a tape to listen to, a friend to have lunch with.
- When you feel especially stressed, let go and do nothing. There are times when "less is more." Instead of taking control and trying to do more to resolve the problem, breathe, meditate, take a walk, do something else. The problem may either solve itself, someone else will handle it or an answer will come to you.
- Avoid extremes. Even good things can be taken too far — recovery, exercise, healthful eating and even fun. Being in touch with the child within does not have to mean becoming a child. Balance leaves us open for many different opportunities, and we can spontaneously choose between good things. We also will occasionally lose it and become compulsive. That's OK too.
- Seek out children. Parents of young children have a built-in balancer; others will need to borrow a friend's

children. My seven-year-old daughter gives me a chance to do things adults are not "supposed" to do — jump rope, play games every day, read great stories, have birthday parties and many more fun things. She has the best ideas and even helps me to pick out clothes that are more fun.

When I look at my children I am conscious that I would not change anything about them. As I grow and feel the child in myself, I can feel the same acceptance of myself.

Spending time with children can be by choice rather than duty or obligation. I have a lot of fun if I choose the best time for me and don't depend only on my daughter's whims. I have my favorite books to read and my favorite games to play. I do it as much for myself, as I do for her.

Affirmations For The Average: A Meditation

One final suggestion to assist in our enjoyment of imperfection is the following meditation. It includes a few affirmations from Shakti Gawain's *Living In The Light* and some of my own.

It would be best if you taped this meditation in your own voice to be played whenever you need a reminder that you are perfect right now:

Relax your body and your mind in whatever way is most comfortable for you. Become conscious of your breathing, letting go of distractions, concerns, tension and noise outside of you. They float away with your breath. Listen to a new, more positive belief system that is growing within you. You are replacing the old messages with something different and unfamiliar to you.

In each of us is an ability and a willingness to learn new things. For this moment you have no need or desire to resist. You feel very open to new information about yourself and others.

The critical voices of your parents, those in authority and your own mental committee are quieted for this moment.

Each day, each moment, you can choose to believe positive messages.

A new voice is developing in you that will soon overcome the critical one.

The child in you is seeking the safety, acceptance and unconditional love this voice will provide.

Listen now to this new affirming voice:

I honor and celebrate my humanness.
My only responsibility is to be true to myself — to be me.
There is no need to be or to act perfectly.
My greatest asset is my honesty, spontaneity and willingness to risk.
I can enjoy being still.
I am supposed to make mistakes — I was made that way.
My humanness makes it easier for others to love me and reach out to me.
What I'm doing is just enough.
My body is beautiful just the way it is.
I can trust my inner voice to tell me what I need.
I am lovable no matter what I do.
I accept myself exactly as I am, for today, this moment.

Knowing When You Are Healthy

Since the goal is not perfection, and we will never truly arrive, how do we know when we are well enough to call ourselves "healthy?" For the most part I believe it is an inner strength, an awareness that we are solidly OK. There are, however, some specific guideposts, which recovering persons have shared and demonstrated throughout the years.

We Feel Choice Over Compulsive Behavior

We are healthy when we are no longer "driven" or obsessed with things. Occasionally we will use compulsiveness to cope. The difference is that we know exactly what we are doing and we are prepared to suffer the consequences without blaming anyone else. We also believe that whether we use food, work, shopping or something else, we eventually will have to deal with the feelings behind them. No one is expected to do it for us. It is not about circumstances making us do it. We are victim to no one but our own choices.

If some aspect of our lives becomes unmanageable, we seek appropriate help and take action. Living in pain is no longer acceptable. I recently received a letter from a recovering co-dependent who has been struggling for years with her nicotine dependence. She had become well enough to quit and wrote, "I've had some difficulty finding the right kind of help so I set up a sort of outpatient rehab for myself, with different therapies, body work and new health and diet regime. It seems like my world has changed — it has inside anyway. This certainly is the biggest event of my recovery."

It is normal to continue to have some struggles in our lives. It is healthy to approach them with choice, a sense of responsibility and hope for progress. When we are healthy, we believe that nothing is beyond our ability to improve. We then choose if and when to work on it.

We Have Incorporated Spirituality Into Daily Living

Being spiritual does not mean being perfect and "God-like." We can have a very healthy spiritual life and make lots of mistakes. I view healthy spirituality as a conscious awareness of our human limitations and an openness to input from both inside ourselves and outside through others. God speaks to us through our inner child, our instincts, our sense of what is right. When we are healthy we seek that inner guidance as easily as we breathe. It is not something we do at a particular time of the day, although that may be part of our expression of spirituality. It is something that is part of everything we do.

When faced with a struggle, a decision, a problem or a conflict, the first thing we do is reflect, pray, look inward or upward, whichever seems right. We no longer strive for control through intellectual means. In health we realize that letting go and reaching out brings more security than trying harder to do more. At times the answer may be simply to live with the problem as it is for now.

When we feel joy or success, there is an appreciation that we are in partnership with something higher than just our own resources. We are not alone on the good days or the bad.

Healthy spirituality may be expressed through organized religion without the expectation that the church, comprised of imperfect people, will be perfect. We do not rigidly adhere to rules without first sifting information through our own belief system and value system. Sometimes we will disagree with what a particular person or church believes to be true. It is not an all-or-nothing matter. We can be an active member of a religious group without accepting all of their beliefs.

I believe that eventually the spiritual person will feel a need to share their spirituality with others through some group experience. Many 12-Step groups have served such a purpose for recovering persons. Others will find an ongoing support system or family where they may openly express this essential part of themselves. Without such expression there may be isolation and doubt. Spirituality grows in numbers, and we will occasionally need to be reminded by others to look for answers from a higher consciousness. The group serves this purpose.

A healthy person can be recognized in a crisis situation as the one who is still centered and at peace. Although we have our ups and downs, there is a higher belief that we are being cared for and that there is meaning and growth in every experience. We know we will be OK no matter what the outcome.

We Feel What We Feel

When we are healthy, there is no sense of urgency to get rid of the feelings we experience. We are comfortable with being angry, afraid, sad or loving. We allow feelings to come and go, without judgment or shame, taking responsibility for our own response to the world. No one causes us to feel or react in a particular way, nor do they need to change to make our bad feelings go away.

When we are angry, we may choose to share it with someone outside of the situation before approaching the source. We are aware that we are not thinking clearly through the anger and do not want to make serious mistakes. When we are sad, we simply may cry or take time to be alone with the feeling before trying to relieve ourselves of it by sharing. We no longer need therapy to get rid of negative feelings, realizing they are a part of healthy living.

We allow friends and family to see us when our feelings are unattractive, but we also are able to use discretion, choosing when not to express ourselves (for example, at work). We are able to postpone expression of pain for the needs of the situation or protection of another such as children, knowing we will get back to it as soon as we can. We then address it by feeling it, talking to someone in our support system or just letting it out.

Feelings are not our enemies, signs of inner disturbance and ill health. They are the substance of who we are: a special, unique, dynamic part of our identity, which we offer to others who share in our lives. We also are tolerant of the feelings of others, seeing them as ever changing, allowing those we love to be responsible for themselves. Although we may never enjoy being around pain, we are willing to listen for the benefit of this person and the growth of the relationship.

We Are Physically Healthy Most Of The Time

None of us will ever perfect the human body, but a healthy person lacks the stress that contributes to illness. We care about our bodies and try to provide the best possible surroundings for our physical and emotional growth. Self-care involves a consciousness of what we ingest, of our need for exercise, of developing problems and a sense of responsibility to do what we need to do for ourselves. It does not involve doing it all perfectly.

In this world it requires great effort to maintain balance between the messages of "you must be perfect" and "the environment is going to kill you anyway." Listening to our bodies and their messages to us helps to make us aware of what we need. Sometimes we choose to listen, sometimes we ignore it; but whatever we do we are making a conscious choice.

Emotionally healthy people probably will have fewer illnesses since positive living is known to affect immunity. This is not about a problem-free life, but about an outlook of hope and a willingness to feel what we feel. Without years of repressed pain, our bodies have a better chance to fight off illness.

We Stretch Ourselves Beyond Who We Are Today

Intellectual growth is an ongoing process of seeking. As healthy people we accept ourselves, but we also desire to learn more, simply for the joy of doing it. In recovery this may mean looking for a new career that better suits your identity, going back to school, seeking a promotion, traveling, finding a mentor or studying international affairs. We are never finished learning.

We are comfortable, although challenged, around those who know more than we do, because we also are aware that we have strengths in other areas. We are comfortable in being the student and try to bring people into our lives who have knowledge or experience that will help us to stretch beyond our present limitations.

We no longer believe that we are supposed to know everything. We pursue only those things that interest or excite us rather than trying to be as good as someone else.

We Have A Solid, Stable Family Of Choice And A Positive Relationship With Our Family Of Origin

Healthy people take responsibility for getting their needs met and have developed a network of support in their lives. This might include a best friend, spouse or lover, sister, a fellow 12-Step group member, a co-worker, a mentor and so on. They probably will not share everything with everyone and may not even see them frequently. They realize that we cannot have ongoing intimate relationships with a large number of people and may feel a sense of fluctuating closeness and distance depending on the present circumstances of their lives.

Family of origin relationships will be based on reality, not on what we would like them to be. Since healthy people are getting their emotional needs met on a regular basis, they do not ask family members to be all things to them. Each family member is seen as an individual, in the present. The decision to risk and be vulnerable with each is based on the safety in that one relationship. Past feelings have been addressed in therapy and there is no need to punish or reject.

Abuse does not exist in the lives of healthy people. They are able to teach others how they wish to be treated, setting limits and expressing feelings as they arise. They are able to reach out and enjoy the good things that exist without resentment about the things that are lacking.

We Feel A Strong Identity Forming

This too is a process, ever changing through developmental stages. There is however a comfort in knowing who we are, a safety in our self-awareness. There are fewer surprises, less vacillating and uncertainty. Others cannot consume us, nor can they take away what we know to be true. "I" statements are easy to make since there is an "I" and we know who that is.

Among the signs of a strong identity is a certainty about our basic needs, even though our wants may change. It is an ability to hold firm to those needs without trying to adapt and live without them. We have preferences and opinions and we express them without fear. Even though we may compromise and negotiate, our beliefs change only when we choose.

We feel connected with our inner child who guides us through her curiosity, inborn abilities and gifts. We do what gives us joy, whether music, sports, running or parenthood, rather than what we feel we are supposed to do. We still have a need for approval, but self-approval is a greater priority. We can risk looking foolish or doing something no one else understands or appreciates.

Our sexual identity has stabilized but continues to grow. We have a stronger sense of our preferences for today, but remain open to the possibilities of tomorrow. No other person can define our sexuality. We feel a personal responsibility for our needs and how we express them.

We Are Able To Balance Work And Play

Balance is an elusive goal in recovery. We are never fully in it, and often fully out of it. As we become healthier, work — the most dangerous area for the perfectionist in the past — changes its focus in our lives. Work becomes a place to go to earn money to feed and clothe ourselves and our families. It is a means to a quality life, not the life itself. Work is not without joy and reward but it is not as important as it once may have been. We may find that although our occupation does not change, our motivation for doing it is significantly different.

When I first began to work as a therapist, I used my work to survive. It provided distraction from the painful life I was living and I thrived on the gratitude of those I treated. The greater the intensity of my work the better I felt. That made working with ACoAs very attractive. As with most compulsions it was not terribly reliable and required more and more stress to maintain the level of intensity I needed. In later recovery I continued to do similar work but I no longer needed the intensity. Since I can feel good about myself when I'm doing less, I don't need my work to be OK. Although I may even be more successful today than in the past, I feel much more calm internally. Ironically, the less I need it, the better I perform.

For many who change careers as they grow, work is more carefully chosen, based on its compatibility with our identity, gifts and life-style. Compromises may be made for many good reasons. Some find more joy in an avocation but keep a particular career for financial rewards or convenience. The dramatic difference is in the degree of choice and in the absence of a victim or "I have to do it" way of thinking. The most important thing is to be true to who you are and that you spend the majority of your time doing something to express who that is.

I recently encountered a cable car conductor in San Francisco who is clearly where he belongs. He is approaching retirement, yet continues to feel and express joy, making others smile as he performs his daily routine after decades of repetition. It doesn't matter what we do, rather how and why we do it.

Many recovering people contemplate becoming a therapist at some point in their early recovery. Before joining any helping profession, however, co-dependents must beware. Although I have the highest regard for my chosen career and my peers, I often meet those who seek a counseling position in the addiction or co-dependency field as a support system for their lives or as an expression of their need to be a caretaker, focused on others. It is very natural to think about giving what you have learned to others; in fact most of us want to do it before we give anything to ourselves. Taking time to recover, while getting to know yourself very well, will prevent serious mistakes.

In health we are learning how to play as well as to balance it with rewarding work. As we let go in one area we make room for opportunities in another. We are able to play without a goal, agenda or planned outcome.

We Are Capable Of Intimacy And Willing To Be Intimate

Whether involved in a committed relationship, seeking one or choosing to be alone, healthy people are well enough to be intimate if they choose. They are not content to live in isolation or superficially with others. They take relationships seriously and do not participate passively when they are in one. Intimacy means more than a sexual connection, and there is a concern both for one's own well-being and that of another.

When we are single we believe that if and when we choose a partner, we are willing to take the risks involved with getting close. We do not enter into close relationships without consciousness of the impact on ourselves and others. There is less fear than before, since we know we have survived before and will be OK.

We worry less about choosing the right person and more about being the right person. It is more important that we concentrate on being truly ourselves and having an honest relationship than to satisfy the other person in order to keep a mediocre one. When we are ourselves, honest and open, capable of intimacy, the process of selection is simplified. Those who are healthy are interested; those who are not, *run*!

We Are Ready To Give It Away To Others

Full recovery does not mean getting totally satisfied with ourselves, but caring about our contribution to making the world a better place. Unlike our co-dependent pattern of giving away what we don't have, we now have more than enough. This contribution comes in many forms, but *nowhere* does it involve diagnosing family or friends and referring them to treatment.

We are ready to accept others as they are while serving as a model of a healthier way to do things. Unlike our former perfectionist selves, we are approachable and real. Our flaws are showing, and so is our self-worth and our feelings. Others find both very attractive and begin to follow without our even noticing.

One day we wake up and notice that our world has changed. There are no more abusive people around us, there is much more humor and joy. People have altered the way they behave around us and possibly even when they aren't around us. We did nothing to make this happen, other than take very good care of ourselves. Letting go has made a difference.

The healthy person feels a sense of awesome responsibility in being blessed with this opportunity to grow and have a richer, more satisfying life. Gratitude replaces resentment for the painful past that brought us to this point. We observe so many others who are hurting and lost without such opportunities. We feel humbled and free and want very much for others to have the same.

The greatest gift many of us can give is to share this beautiful new life with the next generation who will not be recovering from anything, simply living as healthy individuals who will make many improvements over what we did for them.

Our goal, then, is to go full circle: back to where we were headed when we began this journey at birth, enjoying the process and the bumps along the way, being as perfectly imperfect as we can be, making the world a better place for our being in it.

References And Suggested Reading

Ackerman, Robert J. **Perfect Daughters, Adult Daughters Of Alcoholics.** Deerfield Beach, FL: Health Communications, 1989.

Adderholdt-Elliott, Miriam. **Perfectionism, What's Bad About Being Too Good.** Minneapolis: Free Spirit Publishing, 1987. (Great for teens)

Bradshaw, John. **Healing The Shame That Binds You.** Deerfield Beach, FL: Health Communications, 1988.

Carnes, Patrick. **Out of the Shadows: Understanding Sexual Addiction.** Minneapolis: CompCare Publications, 1983.

Clarke, Jeanne Illsley and Dawson, Connie. **Growing Up Again, Parenting Ourselves, Parenting our Children.** San Francisco: Harper & Row, 1989.

Clarke, Jeanne Illsley. **Self-Esteem: A Family Affair.** New York: Harper & Row, 1978.

Gawain, Shakti, with Laurel King. **Living in the Light.** San Rafael, CA: Whatever Publishing, 1986.

Kamiya, Gary. "The Cancer Personality." *Hippocrates, The Magazine of Health and Medicine.* (Nov./Dec., 1989).

Lerner, Rokelle. Pamphlet, *Boundaries for Co-dependents.* Hazelden Foundation, 1988.

Rapoport, Judith L., M.D., **The Boy Who Couldn't Stop Washing, The Experience and Treatment of Obsessive-Compulsive Disorder.** Markham, Ontario: New American Library, 1990.

Sex and Love Addicts Anonymous. Boston: The Augustine Fellowship, Sex and Love Addicts Anonymous, Fellowship-Wide Services, 1986.

Sheppard, Kay. **Food Addiction: The Body Knows.** Deerfield Beach, FL: Health Communications, 1989.

Smith, Ann W. **Grandchildren of Alcoholics: Another Generation of Co-dependents.** Deerfield Beach, FL: Health Communications, 1988.

Stern, Ellen Sue. **The Indispensable Woman.** New York: Bantam Books, 1988.